DISCIPLES OF ALL NATIONS

DISCIPLES OF ALL NATIONS

Your guide to living & understanding the new evangelization

JOSEPHINE LOMBARDI

TWENTY
THIRD 23rd
PUBLICATIONS
www.23rdpublications.com

Cover art:
PENTECOSTÉS
Arete Religioso Contemporáneo/México 1997
By Jaime Domínguez/Fr. Gabriel Ch., OSB

Twenty-Third Publications
1 Montauk Avenue, Suite 200, New London, CT 06320
(860) 437-3012 ◆ (800) 321-0411 ◆ www.23rdpublications.com

ISBN: 978-1-62785-022-3
Library of Congress Catalog Card Number: 2014931232
Printed in the U.S.A.

Table of Contents

Document Abbreviations

AG   *Ad Gentes,* Decree on the Missionary Activity of the Church, 1965.

DH   *Dignitatis Humanae,* Declaration on Religious Freedom, 1965.

EG   *Evangelii Gaudium,* Apostolic Exhortation of Pope Francis, 2013.

EN   *Evangelii Nuntiandi,* Apostolic Exhortation of Pope Paul VI, 1975.

GS   *Gaudium et Spes,* Pastoral Constitution on the Church in the Modern World, 1965.

LG   *Lumen Gentium,* Dogmatic Constitution on the Church, 1964.

RM   *Redemptoris Missio,* Encyclical of John Paul II, On the Permanent Validity of the Church's Missionary Mandate, 1990.

Introduction

As I was watching television the other night, I noticed a show called *Who Do You Think You Are?* While this show is about tracing genealogical roots, the question is appropriate for everyone who is interested in searching for the meaning of life. Many of us do not take the time to think about who we are and who we are called to be.

Examining these questions of course leads to other questions: What is the end goal in life? Why do I exist? Why is God interested in my life? What is God's plan for me?

But these questions are not only for us to answer about ourselves. There is a bigger picture as well. In this book I intend to explore these issues in light of the New Evangelization. Here are some of the questions we will look at:

- What does it mean to evangelize, and why should we do it?

- Is evangelization only the responsibility of priests or religious?

- How does knowing Jesus Christ change people?

- Why is it not enough for Catholics to attend Sunday Mass and then get back to their regular routine?

If we do not take the time to think about these questions and the deeper meaning of our faith, we will miss out on the great joy and peace that come with knowledge of and intimacy with God. Knowledge of God leads to self-knowledge and the end of an identity crisis for Christians.

The Need for Knowledge

The New Evangelization is about knowing God and being known. Knowledge and faith form disciples, and disciples form nations. We evangelize so people can *know* God through an encounter with Jesus Christ. In the book of the prophet Hosea we read, "My people are destroyed for lack of knowledge" (4:6). But before we evangelize, we need knowledge of ourselves. Knowledge of God heals and restores, whereas lack of God-knowledge holds us back and delays spiritual growth. An evangelized person possesses this type of knowledge. Jesus helps us acquire this knowledge. This type of work involves daily reflection and the desire for renewal. An evangelized person knows she is known and knows God with a greater intimacy.

Self-knowledge and Evangelization

St. Augustine came to realize that self-knowledge is key to understanding God's work in your life: "Grant, Lord, that I may know myself that I may know thee," he said. Thomas à Kempis, in his *Imitation of Christ,* says that "a humble self-knowledge is a surer way to God than a search after deep meaning."[1] This self-awareness and self-knowledge reveal the areas of our lives that require pruning and transformation. An encounter with our Lord Jesus Christ deepens this knowledge and reflects back to us the plan God has for our transformation, where we become the best version of ourselves.

Self-knowledge informs our prayer life and builds the humility we need to allow Christ to heal us. St. Teresa of Avila, in her spiritual masterpiece *The Interior Castle,* maps out the soul's journey towards union with God. She uses the image of a castle with seven mansions to describe the details of the journey and the steps that need to be completed to graduate to the next level. With all of the intrigue of the mansions and their unique demands, readers may miss the key insight of her introduction. Before she shares the soul's development in each of the mansions, St. Teresa refers to the courtyard just outside the first mansion. The first mansion has prayer as its lesson, but the soul must master another lesson before entering the first mansion: self-knowledge. St. Teresa says that creatures without self-knowledge are like reptiles, less than human.

If we lack self-knowledge, we do not know what we need, how we should change or what we should improve. We may not know that which we truly desire. Humble self-knowledge coupled with a healthy prayer life leads to an encounter with Jesus Christ, who reveals God and the best of humanity.

The New Evangelization is all about this encounter with the person of Jesus Christ. A wise person once said, "If we can get to people's hearts, their minds and bodies will follow." An encounter with Christ involves a heart connection, not just bodies in the pew or catechized minds. "With hearts transformed by Christ, we can change the hearts of others, and transform the world," Cardinal Wuerl said.[2] This heart knowledge leads to transformation and self-awareness, because self-knowledge and knowledge of God are part of this ongoing process of rediscovering the joy of our faith. The trouble is that many people may be walking around not knowing who they are and what they need.

Sharing the Joy of Being Known by God

Journalist Dan Wooding once asked Blessed Teresa of Calcutta, "What is it like to work with the poorest of the poor?" She responded that she did not work with the poorest of the poor; those in the West are the poorest of the poor:

> The spiritual poverty of the Western World is much greater than the physical poverty of our people ... You, in the West, have millions of people who suffer such terrible loneliness and emptiness. They feel unloved and unwanted. These people are not hungry in the physical sense, but they are in another way. They know they need something more than money, yet they don't know what it is. What they are missing is a living relationship with God.[3]

They are missing joy and are in need of rediscovering the joy of faith, as Pope Benedict XVI explains in his letter announcing the Year of Faith in 2012. "The deepest poverty is the inability of joy, the tediousness of a life considered absurd and contradictory."[4]

The New Evangelization reminds people who they are: children of God who are loved by a God who desires trust and intimacy. Often we do not know or trust that we are known. When we think of the theological virtue of faith, three verbs should come to mind: to believe, to know and to trust. The problem is that many of us limit our understanding of faith to belief. But belief on its own does not reflect the fullness of a complete act of faith. Do we trust God? Do we know God? Do we trust that we are loved and known? These are all important aspects of faith.

> "And this is eternal life, that they may know you, the only true God, and Jesus Christ whom you have sent ... I made your name known to them, and I will make it known, so that the love with which you have loved me may be in them, and I in them."
> Prayer of Jesus ∾ JOHN 17:3, 26

I lost my mother 12 years ago and my father 22 years ago. Sadness overcomes me each time I have the desire to call my mother and share some good news with her, each time I want to call her to lament or process out loud. Not long ago, a friend of mine also lost both her parents. When my friend came over for coffee, she told me how much she missed them. As we shared our common grief and sadness, I asked her, "What do you miss most about your mother?" She replied, "I miss being known. My mother knew me and she knew how to respond to my needs, joys and sorrows."

I often think about her words as I remember my own parents. While many people see me as an extrovert, I have many introvert qualities. I love to be alone and to work alone. I like to withdraw after a public speaking engagement and I enjoy my quiet time with the Lord. When I was 18, I overheard my mother chatting with a neighbour about me. I thought my mother knew me, but I did not realize she knew me so well! The neighbour was commenting on my personality and how I relate to people. My mother said, "Don't let that fool you. Josie loves to be alone. She spends many hours alone on a daily basis." Now that I have four children of my own, I can appreciate my mother's insight into my personality. Of course she knew me. She was my mother.

> "I am the good shepherd; I know my sheep and they know me."
> ∾ JOHN 10:14

As Jesus said in the gospels, what parent would give his child a scorpion or a snake if she was hungry? Surely the child would be given an egg or a fish (Luke 11:11). How much more, therefore, God knows us and loves us.

Of my four children, I could tell you who would unload the dishwasher without being asked, who would have to be asked, and who would have to be bribed. This insight into the human condition and family dynamics should encourage a rethinking of God's love for us. The New Evangelization, as we will discover, is about reminding people that they are loved by a God who knows them. Pope John Paul II, during his 2002 visit to Canada for World Youth Day, spoke of God's love for us. He spoke of his hope that all people would know and experience the love God shares with his Son, Jesus Christ. John Paul II went on to remind us of the real possibility of being the image of Jesus in the world. There are many who belong to the Church, many who are catechized, who may not know this truth. The New Evangelization is about this truth that starts with an encounter with Christ and the salvation he offers.

Where does the Church fit into all this? The Church "exists in order to evangelize" (*Evangelii Nuntiandi*, n. 14), to make known God's will – his loving desire to see us saved and free. Evangelization drives all missionary activity, both within the Church and outside the boundaries of Christianity: "The Church has received this solemn mandate of Christ to proclaim the saving truth from the apostles and must carry it out to the very ends of the earth" (*Lumen Gentium*, n. 17).

1

Evangelization

What Is Evangelization?

"Go therefore and make disciples of all nations, baptizing them in the name of the Father and of the Son and of the Holy Spirit, and teaching them to obey everything that I have commanded you. And remember, I am with you always, to the end of the age."
~ MATTHEW 28:19-20

To evangelize does not mean simply to teach a doctrine, but to proclaim Jesus Christ by one's words and actions, that is, to make oneself an instrument of his presence and action in the world. (Congregation for the Doctrine of the Faith, *Doctrinal Note on Evangelization*, n. 2)

Jesus is the source of all evangelization. Jesus is "the first and greatest evangelizer" (*Evangelii Nuntiandi*, n. 7). The Greek word *euangelion*, which gives us the word "evangelization," means "gospel." The gospel is the "good news" or the "good message." Before the time of Jesus, Roman emperors would send out "good news" or the gospel to their citizens to announce something new or good that was happening. The early gospel writers (the evangelists) adopted this term and applied it to Jesus Christ.

What is the good news for Christians? That Jesus is the saviour of the world. Jesus is the anointed one, the Christ. He is God's Son and our redeemer. The gospel is the story of his life, death and resurrection. This story, once you engage with it and try to live it, changes you forever. Salvation is the change you experience. The New Evangelization inspires a "new you."

Evangelization involves spreading the good news that Jesus gives meaning to our lives and walks with us as we search for truth, love and wholeness. We can proclaim Christ using words and actions, signs and symbols: "in preaching, catechesis, baptism and the administration of the other sacraments" (*Evangelii Nuntiandi*, n. 17). The hope is that people will encounter Christ as they participate in these activities. The goal is "to make oneself an instrument of his presence and action in the world" (CDF, Doctrinal Note, n. 2). In other words, an evangelized person becomes another Christ and inspires others to do the same.

John's Gospel describes Jesus' encounter with the woman of Samaria. She is part of a rival tribe, and contact with anything she touched or served would make a Jew unclean. Jesus could have taken another path to get to his destination, but he passes through Samaria instead, knowing how his community regarded this group. Not only does he ask for a drink, he offers her everlasting life from a source that will quench her thirst for love forever (John 4:1-42). She learns that all other passions leave one thirsty and hungry; he is the only encounter that satisfies. This story reminds us that an encounter with Christ transforms individuals.

A typical search through current TV shows reveals that many people have a distorted sense of pleasure and happiness. One piece of chocolate cake leaves them wanting more sugar; one sexual encounter leaves them wanting more; one promotion increases their desire for success and status. If any one of these actions or habits truly satisfied us, we would stop craving them. But the craving is endless and may seduce us into engaging in habits that are far from life-giving. The New Evangelization offers Christ as the only source of spiritual satisfaction: "We re-propose Christ as the answer to a world staggering under the weight of so many unanswered questions of the heart," says Cardinal Wuerl.[5]

This re-proposing involves a whole range of activity and action the Church is undertaking to spread the gospel message, including the fact that Jesus rose from the dead. The same power that raised him from the dead can redeem our losses, pain and suffering (Romans 8:11). There is hope for a new life in Christ because an encounter with Jesus offers a whole new way of being and living.

Spreading the gospel message also involves word and deed. In fact, by virtue of our baptism, we have no choice but to evangelize, because Jesus commissioned us to do so. The key, however, according to the Decree on Missionary Activity, *Ad Gentes* (1965), is that no one should evangelize who has not been evangelized and converted (n. 40). In other words, you must know the message well.

When a person falls in love, she wants to share the good news with family and friends. No doubt she will describe the love of her life with great joy and satisfaction. When people ask her, "How do you know he's the one?" she will just know. A person in love with the Lord Jesus Christ just knows. She knows him and knows the gift he offers: salvation.

Salvation: The Reason We Evangelize

> The primary reason for evangelizing is the love of Jesus which we have received, the experience of salvation which urges us to ever greater love of him. (Pope Francis, *Evangelii Gaudium*, n. 264)

Salvation can be understood as divine health or restoration. Jesus reveals two mysteries to us; in his divinity, he reveals who God is, and in his humanity, he reveals who we are called to be: the fully restored image and likeness of God. This is why Paul refers to Jesus as the New Adam (Ephesians 2:24; Colossians 3:10). Jesus reveals to us the Father and the image and likeness of God in its perfected form. He is a sneak preview of both mysteries, human and divine.

These were revealed at the transfiguration of Jesus. While we will not experience the glorified state of our being until the second coming of Jesus and the final resurrection, we can experience the process of transformation and conversion in this lifetime as we prepare for the beatific vision, which is union with God. Jesus is salvation. His name means "God's salvation." His name reveals his mission and identity. The universal salvific will of God drives evangelization and missionary activity (1 Timothy 2:4). Our mission and identity is connected to his. If we follow him, we will continue his work.

Announcing the gospel involves announcing God's plan: to see us saved and free. Not only do we re-propose Christ and his gospel, we re-propose the gift of salvation: divine health, or *salus*. The doctrine of salvation was the focus of my study for about ten years. I knew that God desired all people to be saved, and that Jesus is the source of our eternal salvation, but I wanted a deeper understanding of this gift. I often joke with my friends that if I had a lot of money, I would finance a documentary called *Saved* and use it to unpack the rich and deep meaning of this gift using music, images and discussion. Many people know this term, and may even know they need it, but like a gift that has not been unwrapped, they may not be sure what it means for them today. Does it mean going to heaven? Will they experience it in the afterlife?

A careful study of the Hebrew Scriptures and the New Testament reveals that both the verb "to save" and the noun "salvation" are connected to the following:

- Restoration/healing (Luke 8:48)

- Forgiveness (Luke 1:77)

- Deliverance/liberation from harm and evil (Matthew 8:23-27)

- Conversion/doing God's will (Luke 19:1-10)

- Becoming God's adopted sons and daughters (Romans 11:14)

- Eternal life beyond the grave with God (1 Corinthians 3:15)

- Beatific vision: to be satisfied by God (union with God)
  (1 Corinthians 13:12)

- Working out our own salvation (Philippians 2:12)

In his 1995 encyclical, *The Gospel of Life,* Pope John Paul II includes many of the elements listed above in his reflection on salvation:

The salvation wrought by Jesus is the bestowal of life and resurrection. Throughout his earthly life, Jesus had indeed bestowed salvation by healing and doing good to all (cf. Acts 10:38). But his miracles, healings and even his raising of the dead were signs of another salvation, a salvation which consists in the forgiveness of sins, that is, in setting man free from his greatest sickness and in raising him to the very life of God. (n. 50)

Early Christian writers defined salvation as the restoration of the image and likeness of God in us. The image is always there, but the likeness can be disfigured due to pride, arrogance and disobedience. Pope Francis tells us that salvation is the work of God's mercy (*Evangelii Gaudium*, n. 112). Retrieval of the restored state requires grace and faith (Romans 5:1) and involves healing, forgiveness and deliverance from spiritual sickness and radical evil. Hence the expression "divine health." Where are you in the process?

One of my favorite professors once started a philosophy class with this question: "What does it feel like to be in my presence? Am I obnoxious, abusive and unapproachable? Or am I loving, kind and approachable?" Love and grace restores the likeness. We can be fed by the loving presence of another. In Italian, we have this saying that a good-natured person is like a "piece of bread." (It sounds better in Italian!) This expression implies the goodness of the person because the person satisfies and feeds with his presence. There is something whole and wholesome about this person. So when we speak of God desiring the salvation of all people, we are talking about God desiring his wholeness for us: restoration and healing. In other words, salvation involves becoming a new person – a new creation.

I like to define salvation as the fulfillment of the Lord's Prayer in individuals, communities and in all of God's creation, in this lifetime and the next. I developed this insight because the Lord's Prayer contains all of the scriptural elements of the deeper meaning of salvation. Pope Paul VI, in his post-synodal apostolic exhortation *Evangelii Nuntiandi*, says this about salvation:

Christ proclaims salvation as the outstanding element and, as it were, the central point of his good news. This is the great gift of God which is to be considered as comprising not merely *liberation from all those things by which man is oppressed* but especially *liberation from sin and from the domination of the evil one, a liberation which incorporates that gladness enjoyed by every man who knows God and is known by him, who sees God and who surrenders himself trustingly to him.* (n. 9, italics added)

Salvation, for Pope Paul VI, involves liberation and joy that come with knowing God and being known. The message of evangelization is salvation: it is a gift offered by God to all people. Jesus Christ is the eternal source of salvation and it is through the "grace and mercy" of God that we can come to experience this great gift. The beginning of this gift can be experienced in this lifetime, but it achieves "its consummation in eternity" (EN, n. 27).

If Jesus is a sneak preview of the Father and restored humanity, it is the power of the Holy Spirit that makes us a sneak preview of Christ. Jesus reveals humanity fully alive and free in the divinized state. This means we are created in the image and likeness of God with the real possibility of being like God. The good news is that Jesus shows us how to be like God: "Be perfect, therefore, as your heavenly Father is perfect" (Matthew 5:48). This call to perfection is a call to participate in the wholeness of God.

> Jesus is "the new man " (cf. **Eph** 4:24; **Col** 3:10) who calls redeemed humanity to share in his divine life. The mystery of the Incarnation lays the foundations for an anthropology which, reaching beyond its own limitations and contradictions, moves towards God himself, indeed towards the goal of " divinization ". This occurs through the grafting of the redeemed on to Christ and their admission into the intimacy of the Trinitarian life. The Fathers have laid great stress on this soteriological dimension of the mystery of the Incarnation: it is only because the Son of God truly became man that man, in him and through him, can truly become a child of God.
> ᴄ◡ POPE JOHN PAUL II, *NOVO MILLENIO INEUNTE*, N. 23

The New Evangelization is all about proclaiming this mystery: Do you know who you are? Do you know that an encounter with Christ will reveal who you are called to be – the best version of yourself? The "New You"? In Christ, "all humanity regains its original and true identity" (*Gaudium et Spes*, n. 22/*Instrumentum Laboris*, n. 11). This is why Jesus commissioned his followers to go out to baptize and preach the good news: all humanity is restored in Jesus Christ.

To evangelize is to communicate an encounter that will leave you transformed. This transformation spills over into our communities: "Whenever a community receives the message of salvation, the Holy Spirit enriches its culture with the transforming power of the Gospel" (EG, n. 116). New studies are confirming our belief that faith changes the whole person. (In Chapters 5 and 6, we will examine some of the exciting research supporting this claim.) The Church's evangelizing efforts have attempted to make this point throughout the centuries. All are called to participate in the wholeness of God; Jesus is the way to this wholeness. The Second Vatican Council emphasized this universal call to holiness; there is no hierarchy of states of life. God has a plan for all individuals who seek him and his will. When it comes to discerning vocations and the call to holiness, our prayer should be: "Lord, lead us to the state of life that will keep us close to you." Pope John Paul II affirmed this call in 2001:

It is necessary therefore to rediscover the full practical significance of Chapter 5 of the Dogmatic Constitution on the Church *Lumen Gentium*, dedicated to the "universal call to holiness". The Council Fathers laid such stress on this point, not just to embellish ecclesiology with a kind of spiritual veneer, but to make the call to holiness an intrinsic and essential aspect of their teaching on the Church. The rediscovery of the Church as "mystery", or as a people "gathered together by the unity of the Father, the Son and the Holy Spirit", was bound to bring with it a rediscovery of the Church's "holiness", understood in the basic sense of belonging to him who is in essence the Holy One, the "thrice Holy" (cf. *Is* 6:3). To profess the Church as holy means to point to her as *the Bride of Christ*, for whom he gave himself precisely in order to make her holy (cf. *Eph* 5:25-26). This as it were objective gift of holiness is offered to all the baptized. (*Novo Millenio Ineunte*, n. 30)

The Nicene Creed teaches that the Church is holy. While this is true, at the same time we are always striving for holiness. Holiness is a possibility for all, not just the few. Different people in different times and places have heard the gospel preached. The challenge is to win people's hearts, not just their bodies and minds. Even if you memorize the whole *Catechism of the Catholic Church*, but have not experienced an encounter with Christ, you are not evangelized, because the love of Christ conquers hearts. A change in heart and character indicates that an encounter with Jesus Christ has taken place.

> "Those who accept his offer of salvation are set free from sin, sorrow, inner emptiness and loneliness." ∞ POPE FRANCIS, *EVANGELII GAUDIUM*, N. 1

St. Paul's conversion illustrates this point. He was a man of arrogance and great intellect, "all puffed up," to use his own words. His training as a Pharisee ensured that he knew things about God, but his training could not guarantee that he would know God intimately. It was his encounter with the Risen Christ that led to his intimate knowledge of God. That encounter informed his ecclesiology, his theological anthropology and his understanding of love as the greatest gift. He may have been born and raised in a religious tradition, but he hears the good news for the first time through his encounter with Christ, because Jesus re-proposed God's love to him. Jesus revealed the dignity of all people to him, a reminder that all are created in God's image and likeness. Some need to hear the message for the first time, while others need it re-proposed. That is the distinction between what we call the First Evangelization and the New Evangelization.

The First Evangelization

The First Evangelization refers to the first proclamation "directed primarily towards those who have never heard the good news of Jesus" (*Evangelii Nuntiandi*, n. 52). This is the proclamation "of Christ our Lord to those who do not know him" (EN, n. 17). Evangelization involves an experience of Jesus and knowing him as a result. Joseph Cardinal Ratzinger, in his Address to Catechists and Religion Teachers of December 12, 2000, affirmed the three key elements of evangelization: the kingdom of God, Jesus Christ, and eternal life. Later, as Pope Benedict XVI, he spoke of three essential elements in the life of the church: "The Church's deepest nature is expressed in her threefold responsibility of proclaiming the word of God (*kerygma-martyria*), celebrating the sacraments (*leitourgia*), and exercising the ministry of charity (*diakonia*)" (*Deus Caritas Est*, n. 25).

Fellowship is the fruit of the Church's engagement of its threefold responsibility. Since the events of the Book of the Acts of the Apostles – Pentecost, the beginning of the First Evangelization – the disciples of Jesus have preached the kingdom of God, fellowship with one another and with Jesus Christ, and the gift of eternal life. They have done this using a variety of methods so that the word of God is proclaimed, sacraments are celebrated, and the vulnerable are fed and served. While many missionaries proclaimed the gospel with good intentions, lack of heart knowledge of Christ and cultural tensions led to many in far-off lands not receiving the fullness of the gospel message. Sometimes the mind leads the body to perform certain functions, to participate in public prayer and ritual, but the heart remains untouched.

With the Europeans' arrival in the New World in 1492, the Church was faced with a new challenge: evangelizing persons living in faraway lands. At this point, the salvation of one's soul depended not only on good works and remaining in a state of grace, but on baptism and explicit faith in Jesus Christ as well. Missionaries felt the pressure of the possibility of damnation for these non-evangelized souls. The methods and means by which these missionaries evangelized, however, created some tension and the need to reconsider whether the gospel was being preached in a convincing way.[6] Pope Alexander VI offered parts of the New World in the west to Spain, and parts of the east to Portugal. (At one point the Diocese of Lisbon, Portugal, spread as far east as China.)

Christianity had now spread past Europe and Asia Minor. While many were brought to Christ and full membership in the Church, modern popes have acknowledged some of the hurt and loss endured by Indigenous peoples during this period. Conquistadors and missionaries worked side by side, leading several missionaries to examine their consciences and their approach to evangelization. In Goa, India, there was the report of a Goan convert to Catholicism who said, "I have cut my hair, I am now wearing trousers, I have a Portuguese last name. What else must I do in order to be Catholic?"

The struggle to preach the gospel in a convincing way, coupled with the desire to bring people into the Church that offers salvation, raised certain ethical questions around freedom and conscience. While the gospel was being preached and advanced in many places, this is good; other factors led to suffering and confusion.

Today, it is very clear that religious freedom is to be respected and honoured in all missionary activity. "It is not by proselytizing that the Church grows, but by attraction" (EG, n. 14). Evangelization is to be distinguished from proselytism. In a doctrinal note, the Congregation for the Doctrine of the Faith (2007) defined proselytism this way: "The promotion of a religion by using means, and for motives, contrary to the spirit of the gospel; that is, which do not safeguard the freedom and dignity of the human person." While we cannot use force or coercion in our evangelizing efforts, we can still respect the freedom of others while making an offer in our proclamation:

> It is certainly wrong to force anything on the conscience of our broth-
> ers. But it is quite another matter to present to their conscience
> the gospel of truth and salvation in Jesus Christ clearly, while fully
> respecting their freedom of choice and election- "excluding every
> form of action which appears to savour of coercion, or dishonest or
> undue persuasion." (EN, n. 80)[7]

It is not a crime to proclaim the beauty of the gospel with the hope that an individual accepts it freely and lovingly, just as we can tell someone we love them but not force them to love us back. Only love freely given and received ensures conversion and joy.

> "This is eternal life, that they may know you, the only true God and
> Jesus Christ whom you have sent" (Jn 17:3). God has given human
> beings intellect and will so that they might freely seek, know and love
> him. Therefore, human freedom is both a resource and a challenge
> offered to man by God who has created him: an offer directed to the

human person's capacity to know and to love what is good and true. Nothing puts in play human freedom like the search for the good and the true, by inviting it to a kind of commitment which involves fundamental aspects of life. This is particularly the case with salvific truth, which is not only an object of thought, but also an event which encompasses the entire person – intelligence, will, feelings, actions and future plans – when a person adheres to Christ. In the search for the good and the true, the Holy Spirit is already at work, opening the human heart and making it ready to welcome the truth of the Gospel, as Thomas Aquinas stated in his celebrated phrase: *omne verum a quocumque dicatur a Spiritu Sancto est.* It is important therefore to appreciate this action of the Spirit, who creates an affinity for the truth and draws the human heart towards it, by helping human knowledge to mature both in wisdom and in trusting abandonment to what is true. (Congregation for the Doctrine of the Faith, *Doctrinal Note on Evangelization,* n. 4)

"The church … has the obligation and the sacred right to evangelize" (*Ad Gentes*, n. 7). The truth is, however, that two thirds of the world's population is not Christian. Of the third that is Christian, one half is Catholic. The gospel took root in Europe, Asia Minor, parts of Africa and in North and South America, while the Far East did not embrace Christianity in the same way. Over the centuries, the magisterium has developed its understanding of salvation outside the Church. The development of this understanding has unfolded over the centuries, as we will see in Chapter 2.

The Teaching of Vatican II and What Happened After the Council

Salvation Outside the Church

On the one hand, the magisterium teaches the duty and obligation to evangelize (*Ad Gentes*, n. 7). On the other hand, it offers an explanation for how people can experience salvation outside the visible boundaries of the Church. The Second Vatican Council (1962–1965) offered a summary of this development that was centuries in the making:

> Finally, those who have not yet received the Gospel are related in various ways to the people of God. In the first place we must recall the people to whom the testament and the promises were given and from whom Christ was born according to the flesh. On account of their fathers this people remains most dear to God, for God does not repent of the gifts He makes nor of the calls He issues. But the plan of salvation also includes those who acknowledge the Creator. In the first place amongst these there are the Muslims, who, professing to hold the faith of Abraham, along with us adore the one and merciful God, who on the last day will judge mankind. Nor is God far distant from those who in shadows and images seek the unknown

God, for it is He who gives to all men life and breath and all things, and as Saviour wills that all men be saved. Those also can attain to salvation who through no fault of their own do not know the Gospel of Christ or His Church, yet sincerely seek God and moved by grace strive by their deeds to do His will as it is known to them through the dictates of conscience. Nor does Divine Providence deny the helps necessary for salvation to those who, without blame on their part, have not yet arrived at an explicit knowledge of God and with His grace strive to live a good life. Whatever good or truth is found amongst them is looked upon by the Church as a preparation for the Gospel. She knows that it is given by Him who enlightens all men so that they may finally have life. But often men, deceived by the Evil One, have become vain in their reasonings and have exchanged the truth of God for a lie, serving the creature rather than the Creator. Or some there are who, living and dying in this world without God, are exposed to final despair. Wherefore to promote the glory of God and procure the salvation of all of these, and mindful of the command of the Lord, "Preach the Gospel to every creature", the Church fosters the missions with care and attention. (*Lumen Gentium*, n. 16)

The above paragraph from *Lumen Gentium* comes after the teaching that other Christians are joined to the Body of Christ by virtue of their baptism. But here it teaches that members of other faiths are related to the Body of Christ and can be saved in Jesus Christ as they seek to do God's will "as they know it through the dictates of conscience." Jesus Christ is the eternal source of salvation for all people, whether they know him or not. The "fullness of the means of salvation" is in the Catholic Church, but there are elements of truth and sanctification in other Christian communities (LG, n. 8).

Some have arrived at an explicit knowledge of God, while others – perhaps due to ignorance, for which they cannot be held responsible – have yet to arrive at an explicit knowledge of God. The truth and good that is found in these communities can serve as a "preparation for the gospel" (*Ad Gentes*, n. 2). The possibility for salvation for those outside the boundaries of the Church does not mean that we stop evangelizing![8] We want people to experience Christ and the fullness of the means of salvation, whether they are Catholic Christians or not. The final section of *Lumen Gentium* n. 16 reminds Christians that the evil one can tempt people to deny God's existence or the need for God. This can lead people to despair, and stop them from reaching out to God for assistance. The fullness of the truth and the gospel need to be proclaimed because we have the duty to make this known. We cannot encourage the thinking that you can live without God.

The Second Vatican Council: The Decree on Missionary Activity, *Ad Gentes*, 1965

Missionary activity, catechetical activity and pastoral activity make up the church's evangelizing mission.[9] Vatican II emphasized the need for ongoing missionary activity. "Missions" refers to that activity involving "heralds" of the gospel who go out and preach the gospel throughout the world, planting churches among people who do not know or believe in Jesus Christ. The "primary purpose" of missionary activity is evangelization, and the "chief means" is preaching the gospel (AG, n. 6).

"In this missionary activity of the Church, various stages are sometimes found side by side: first, that of the beginning or planting, then that of newness or youth" (AG, n. 6).

> This missionary activity derives its reason from the will of God, "who wishes all men to be saved and to come to the knowledge of the truth. For there is one God, and one mediator between God and men, Himself a man, Jesus Christ, who gave Himself as a ransom for all" (1 Tim. 2:45); "neither is there salvation in any other" (Acts 4:12) (AG, n. 7).

The following are key points made by this important document:

- All must be converted to Jesus Christ (proposing, not imposing or using force or coercion). (n. 7)

- Faith, baptism and the church are necessary. (n. 7)

- Members of the Church have a sacred duty to preach the gospel. (n. 7)

- Christ reveals to all people "the real truth about their condition and their whole calling." (n. 8)

- The whole church is missionary by nature. (n. 35)

- Evangelization is a basic duty of the People of God. (n. 35)

- "Interior renewal" reveals an awareness of one's own responsibility for preaching and spreading the gospel. (n. 35)

By virtue of our baptism, we are all called to be missionaries, but we need to be evangelized ourselves before we can begin to bring Christ to others. The teaching of the Council went on to inspire the teaching of future popes and synods. Pope Paul VI, the pope who closed the Second Vatican Council in 1965, explored these levels in his apostolic exhortation *Evangelii Nuntiandi* (1975):

Levels of Evangelization

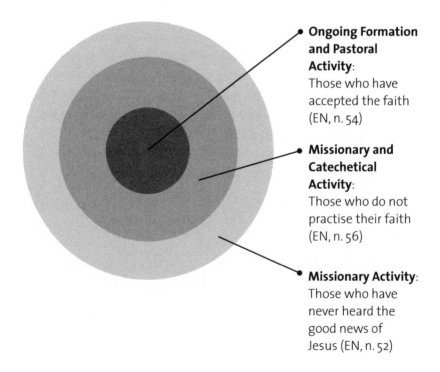

Ongoing Formation and Pastoral Activity:
Those who have accepted the faith (EN, n. 54)

Missionary and Catechetical Activity:
Those who do not practise their faith (EN, n. 56)

Missionary Activity:
Those who have never heard the good news of Jesus (EN, n. 52)

THOSE WHO HAVE NOT HEARD THE GOOD NEWS OF JESUS: THE CALL FOR MISSIONARY ACTIVITY

"The New Evangelization is a call to the Church to rediscover her missionary origins." ∾ *INSTRUMENTUM LABORIS*, N. 81

This is part of the first proclamation or the first evangelization. As stated in *Nostra Aetate*, the Declaration on the Relation of the Church to Non-Christian Religions (1965), the Church rejects nothing that is "true and holy" in other religious traditions; however, the magisterium is clear that Christ is to be preached everywhere. The New Evangelization has not changed anything regarding the need to evangelize outside the visible boundaries of Christianity. Jesus reveals God in his divinity and the best version of humanity in his humanity. "Jesus Christ reveals man to himself" (GS 22). It is our understanding of theological anthropology, or what it means to be human and Christian, that informs our missionary efforts. Missionary activity, according to Pope Francis, is not about self-preservation, it is about transforming everything:

> I dream of a "missionary option", that is, a missionary impulse capable of transforming everything, so that the Church's customs, ways of doing things, times and schedules, language and structures can be suitably channeled for the evangelization of today's world rather than for her self-preservation. (EG, n. 27)

Jesus reveals the true face of God and invites everyone to experience an intimate relationship with God. Although non-Christians can be saved through the grace that God bestows in "ways known to him" (*Gaudium et Spes*, n. 22), knowing Jesus reveals truth regarding God's plan for human nature. In a *Doctrinal Note on Evangelization*, the Congregation for the Doctrine of the Faith reveals the benefit of knowing Jesus Christ, the true face of God (n. 7). The friendship offered by Christ reminds us that God is with us. Knowing Christ brings freedom, exalts human nature and "directs" the person towards his or her fulfillment (n. 7). "The Church wants everyone to share in these goods so that they may possess the fullness of truth and the fullness of the means of salvation..." (n. 7). These spiritual goods lead one to the fullness of truth and a greater intimacy with God. Many missionaries have dedicated their lives to the spread of the gospel. Their efforts have contributed to the development of communities, giving people access to resources, and witnessing to the love of Jesus Christ. The Congregation for the Evangelization of Peoples is a Vatican office that deals with the evangelization of those outside the boundaries of Christianity.

> "People in this type of soil do not have faith in Jesus Christ as the Son of God, risen from the dead. They may have heard something about him ... but their lives have not been changed by him. They have not encountered Jesus in a personal, life-giving and saving way."
> ∾ ON GOOD SOIL: PASTORAL PLANNING FOR EVANGELIZATION AND CATECHESIS WITH ADULTS, P. 45

We continue to preach Jesus Christ to all people because Jesus reveals our present condition to us and shows us the possibility of becoming the best version of ourselves, another Christ. We propose, not impose, the following revelation: It is remarkable that we have a God who became one of us so that we can be like him. This is Good News!

THOSE WHO HAVE ACCEPTED THE FAITH: THE CALL FOR FORMATION AND PASTORAL ACTIVITY

> "The Church is an evangelizer, but she begins by being evangelized herself." ∾ INSTRUMENTUM LABORIS, N. 37

Practising Catholics, both lay people and clergy, need to be fed with the word and the sacraments. Their evangelization consists of ongoing formation. Some may require basic catechesis, while others may need more advanced study and formation. This category consists not only of those who are nourished by Christ's word and flesh, but also those who "seldom take part in worship" (EG, n. 14). These individuals need pastoral ministry that will engage them and encourage them to grow spiritually. The goal is to assist them so that they can "respond to God's love ever more fully in their lives" (EG, n. 14).

The goal of catechetical activity "is to deepen the individual's relationship with Jesus Christ in and through the Church. This is best described as an apprenticeship in the Christian life."[10] It would be helpful for pastors and lay ministers to organize a library of books and multimedia resources that engage people at different levels of learning and expertise. An encyclical may feed some, while starving and frustrating others. Those who are spiritually mature may need ongoing pastoral supports and encouragement to be involved in a number of ways. They may be ready to take on a greater responsibility in the evangelization of others.[11]

> "The Church always evangelizes and has never interrupted the path of evangelization. She celebrates the Eucharistic mystery every day, administers the sacraments, proclaims the word of life—the Word of God, and commits herself to the causes of justice and charity. And this evangelization bears fruit: it gives light and joy, it gives the path of life to many people; many others live, often unknowingly, of the light and the warmth that radiate from this permanent evangelization."
> ∾ JOSEPH CARDINAL RATZINGER, ADDRESS TO CATECHISTS AND RELIGION TEACHERS, DECEMBER 12, 2000

Those in this category are called to continual renewal. I often joke that I feel as though I have been different people throughout my journey. Just when I think the growing has stopped, I am humbled or reminded of the need to grow and be transformed. A new lesson presents itself or I feel challenged and stretched. The process of transformation is lifelong, and we need humility and self-knowledge to continue. God's grace reminds us that we are not alone, and is sufficient to help us make it through good times and bad. Access to resources and various workshops is a must for the people in this category.

At St. Augustine's Seminary in Scarborough, Ontario, we have introduced a new lay formation program. We offer days of formation related to the four pillars of formation that shape the training of seminarians:

• Human Formation (growing in self-awareness/transformation)

- Spiritual Formation (knowledge of God/mature prayer life)

- Pastoral Formation (pastoral care/ministry formation)

- Intellectual Formation (the academic study of our faith)

The Second Vatican Council affirmed the baptism of all the faithful, calling all Catholics to live out their baptismal promises. By virtue of our baptism, we are invited to participate in the mission of Jesus Christ (Mt. 28:19). We are all "agents of evangelization" (EG, n. 120). The formation of lay people was encouraged and programs were developed for the study of theology and other related disciplines. Many have rejoiced and flourished as a result of the invitation to be formed for professional ministry. While the pillars of intellectual and pastoral formation have been included in the training of lay people, many desire more human and spiritual formation. The four pillars of formation should be included in any plan to catechize and minister to those in this category.

Catholics are encouraged to contact their local chanceries and diocesan websites to learn about any courses or centres of formation that are available to them. Some opportunities are available through their parishes, while others may be offered through their diocesan office, retreat houses or local colleges or universities. The chapter on Witness and Proclamation and the chapter on the Seven Sectors will continue to address ways in which members of this group can grow in their faith and touch the lives of those who should know Christ or do not know him. *This group of individuals will be used by the Holy Spirit to evangelize those in the first and next category.*

THOSE WHO DO NOT PRACTISE THEIR FAITH – THE CONVERSION OF THE BAPTIZED: A CALL FOR MISSIONARY AND CATECHETICAL ACTIVITY

Imagine a couple who has been married for over 30 years who have lived many of those years in silence, communicating at a distance, not really knowing one another. Not knowing what the other loves to do, or the other's preference for movies, music, restaurants. A couple of times each year, they may go out for dinner for birthdays or anniversaries, but there is no real depth of intimacy. Each feels that something is missing but cannot name it. There is no joy, nor satisfaction in this relationship.

Now imagine that this relationship is between a person and Jesus. Many Catholics who have been baptized and who have received other sacraments may be showing up at Mass from time to time without any joy or satisfaction – it is obligation or duty that drives their minimal involvement. They may even know things about Jesus, but do not know him as a person. Nor do they know that they are known by God in an intimate way, the way they may know their loved ones. They have not been changed by this encounter. The New Evangelization seeks to deepen the faith of those who practise their faith, but most importantly, it seeks to re-propose the gospel of Jesus so that people can rediscover the joy of his presence. The New Evangelization is all about deepening our faith, "gaining confidence in the truth of that faith and sharing with others."[12]

The transformation of those people in category two will inspire the transformation of those in this category. Pope Francis names three evils that have hurt our evangelizing efforts. These evils, he says, led to the decline of joy in our communities:

> Today we are seeing in many pastoral workers, including consecrated men and women, an inordinate concern for their personal freedom and relaxation, which leads them to see their work as a mere appendage to their life, as if it were not part of their very identity. At the same time, the spiritual life comes to be identified with a few religious exercises which can offer a certain comfort but which do not encourage encounter with others, engagement with the world or a passion for evangelization. As a result, one can observe in many agents of evangelization, even though they pray, a heightened individualism, a crisis of identity and a cooling of fervor. These are three evils which fuel one another. (EG, n. 78)

It appears that Pope Francis is challenging those in category two to avoid these three evils because they stifle the work of the Holy Spirit. ***The evangelization of members of category three depends on the evangelizing efforts of those in category two.*** They need people who are filled with joy and fervor to communicate the gift of salvation and the gift of knowing Jesus Christ. John Paul II once said that "many of the baptized live as if Christ did not exist: the gestures and signs of faith are repeated, especially in devotional practices, but they fail to

35

correspond to a real acceptance of the content of the faith and fidelity to the person of Jesus" (*Ecclesia in Europa*, n. 47).

It will be in an encounter with Christ in the various sectors that make up our global community that will evangelize those who should know Christ. It will be an encounter with Christ in preaching that will inspire a conversion. (Later we will explore the need for "prepared" preaching and how homilies and reflections can touch people and spark an interest in their faith.) Lastly, it will be an encounter with Christ in the "new you" that will inspire an interest in Christ and the desire to be formed as a disciple. These encounters will encourage a return to the Church, where one can continue to be fed with Christ's word and the sacraments. We will explore these encounters in upcoming chapters.

What's "New" about the New Evangelization?

"See, I am making all things new." ∞ REVELATION 21:5

We need "new ways of relating to God" (EG, n. 74). This involves a new approach to presenting or reproposing Jesus Christ, who "is the same yesterday and today and forever" (Heb. 13:8). The message and the person of Jesus Christ are not new, but an encounter with him may be new for some people. This encounter leads to another type of newness: the "new you." Jesus will make you "new" or restore you to divine health. The New Evangelization proposes newness at many levels, individual and communal. In order to achieve this newness, this evangelization is to be new in ardour, methods and expression:

> The conditions of society today require us all to *revise our methods and to seek out with all our energy new ways and means by which the Christian message may be brought to the men of our times,* for it is only in this message that they can find the answer to their doubts and the inspiration to carry out the obligations arising from their mutual dependency (Pope Paul VI, Address to College of Cardinals, June 22, 1973, in *Evangelii Nuntiandi*, n. 3, emphasis mine.)

Pope John Paul II continued this vision by referring to new ardour, methods and expressions in a number of addresses and documents. We will consider these documents in chapters 4, 5 and 6.

WHAT IS ARDOUR?

- Warmth and enthusiasm
- Energy and joy
- Love for the Lord

EXAMPLES OF METHODS (WAYS OF EVANGELIZING)

- Preaching: feeding with the word (EN, n. 42–43)

- Catechetical instruction (EN, n. 44): Solid catechesis consists of a consideration of the theological foundations for the New Evangelization:

  » anthropological: We are created in the image and likeness of God.

  » Christological: Jesus reveals God in his divinity, and restored humanity in his humanity. We are called to partake in his divinity and be fully restored.

  » ecclesiological: We are the Body of Christ: many members with a variety of gifts inspired by the Holy Spirit.

  » soteriological: God desires the salvation of all people: that we receive divine health and become the best version of ourselves. This is the way to becoming another Christ. (see Cardinal Donald Wuerl, *New Evangelization: Passing on the Catholic Faith Today*, pp. 78–79)

- Scripture study

- Sacramental preparation and reception (EN, n. 47)

- Personal testimonies (EN, n. 46)

- Popular piety (EN, n. 48)

- Community events

- Building of a multimedia parish library

- Distribution of flyers, booklets[13]

- Calls into talk shows or letters to the media whenever the Church is misrepresented

- Charitable acts

- Media and social communications (EN, n. 45)

- Encounters with Christ in various sectors[14]

- Ongoing formation of clergy, religious and laity

"Of course we must use the modern methods of making ourselves heard in a reasonable way – or better yet: of making the voice of the Lord accessible and comprehensible." ❧ JOSEPH CARDINAL RATZINGER, ADDRESS TO CATECHISTS AND RELIGION TEACHERS, DECEMBER 12, 2000

EXPRESSIONS (HOW TO MAKE CHRIST KNOWN)

- A missionary spirituality (desire to share Christ with all people)

- Conversion and self-knowledge (change in character)

- Renewal of human nature (EN, n. 24) (becoming the best version of ourselves)

- Love of neighbour (assisting others with their daily needs)

- Witness and proclamation (EN, n. 24) (proclaiming Christ with word and deed)

- Entrance into a community of faith (EN, n. 24) (initiation of new Christians/catechesis)

- Witness of clergy, religious and lay people (EN, n. 24) (ongoing formation and spiritual growth/being a sign of salvation)

- Pastoral care/apostolic works (EN, n. 24) (ministering to the sick or afflicted)

"To speak of a new evangelization does not in fact mean that a single formula should be developed that would hold the same for all circumstances." ∾ POPE BENEDICT XVI, 2010

Pope Paul VI summarized the teaching objective of the Second Vatican Council: "to ensure that the church of the 20th century may emerge ever better equipped to proclaim the gospel to people of this century" (*Evangelii Nuntiandi*, n. 2). Being better equipped, according to Cardinal Ratzinger, includes handing on the right content of our faith. He lists four essentials:

1. Conversion
2. Kingdom of God
3. Jesus Christ
4. Eternal life[15]

These essentials remind us that the New Evangelization is deeply Christocentric: focused on Christ. The *General Directory for Catechesis* lists five criteria for catechesis and evangelization that ensure the gospel is presented "with integrity and authenticity."[16] The presence of these criteria in missionary, catechetical and pastoral activity affirms that the gospel is being faithfully transmitted. Here is a summary of the five criteria:

CRITERIA NEEDED IN CATECHESIS AND EVANGELIZATION

- Missionary, Catechetical and Pastoral Activity is to be Christocentric and Trinitarian.
- Belief that the Gospel we share is Good News
- The salvation and liberation offered by Jesus is proclaimed in the present context.
- Jesus' message of redeeming love is intended for all people.
- The Gospel message is to be presented in its entirety.[17]

The above criteria remind us that we cannot evangelize without referring to Christ. In showing that Jesus brings liberation and loves all people, we re-propose authentic freedom. The gospel message leads us to truth and salvation. This message, as the criteria notes, needs to be proclaimed in all contexts.

> "Every form of authentic evangelization is always " new "...The real newness is the newness which God himself mysteriously brings about and inspires, provokes, guides and accompanies in a thousand ways."
> ∾ POPE FRANCIS, *EVANGELII GAUDIUM*, NN. 11, 12

The "New" in New Evangelization not only refers to ardour, methods and expression; it also refers to new times, new cultures, new contexts and creating a new people. "The adjective 'new' refers to a cultural situation which has changed the need for the Church, with renewed energy, determination, resourcefulness and newness, to look at the way she lives and transmits the faith" (*Instrumentum Laboris*, n. 49). The New Evangelization, however, "does not mean a new Gospel" (n. 164). It means an adequate response to the signs of the times, to the needs of people living in today's social and cultural context. How we transmit the faith must pay attention to cultural and demographic trends and developments. The "New Evangelization" is to tap into new methods and expressions, making the gospel more accessible and comprehensible in all contexts and cultures throughout the world, taking into consideration the needs of all people. While Pope Paul VI referred to new approaches and levels of evangelization in 1975 (an evangelization that is new), the expression "the new evangelization" was first heard in a document produced by the bishops of Latin America who gathered in Puebla, Mexico in 1979:

> New situations, emerging from socio-cultural changes require a *new evangelization*: emigrants to other countries, large urban conglomerates in our own countries, masses from all levels of society in a precarious situation as to the faith, groups exposed to the influence of sects and of ideologies which do not respect their identity, causing confusion and provoking division.[18]

These situations, coupled with demographic shifts and developments, have pushed the Church to respond to new challenges arising in places that were predominantly Catholic Christian.

3

Demographics
and Evangelization

"Vast demographic shifts in the Catholic population are reconfiguring the face of the Church and shifting the institution's center from its historic European heartland." ᴏᴠ JONATHAN LUXMOORE, "DEMOGRAPHIC SHIFTS MEAN EUROPE NO LONGER CATHOLIC CHURCH'S CENTER," *CATHOLIC NEWS SERVICE*, APRIL 10, 2013

The Global Christian Forum, a gathering of leaders from all major Christian communities and world communions, met in Manado, Indonesia, in October 2011 to address trends and shifts in global Christianity. The membership consisted of representatives from the Anglican Communion, World Council of Churches, World Evangelical Alliance, Pentecostal World Fellowship and the Vatican's Pontifical Council for the Promotion of Christian Unity. The presenters shared that the story of worldwide Christianity is being rewritten before our eyes, and noted the various cultural and demographic shifts that have occurred over the past hundred years. The statistical analysis of changing demographics and practices of global Christianity revealed the following trends:

- In 1910, 66% of the world's Christians lived in Europe.

- Today, Europe accounts for only 26% of the world's Christian population.

- The global North (Europe and North America) consisted of over 80% Christians in 1910, falling to under 40% in 2010.

- In 1910, less than 2% of all Christians lived in Africa; this rose to 20% by 2010.

- The statistical centre of gravity for global Christianity has shifted from near Madrid to south of Timbuktu in Mali.

- This 100-year shift is the most dramatic in Christian history.

In Canada, a recent census revealed that 43% of the Canadian population consists of baptized Catholics: as of 2008, that means 13,070,000 people.[19] In the United States, a study conducted by the Pew Forum on Religion and Public Life found that 78.4% of the US population claims to be Christian. Thirty-one percent were raised in the Catholic faith; however, 24% describe themselves as Catholic.[20]

In a study of faith practices in Canada (2011), Rick Hiemstra, who works in the area of research and media relations, looked at affiliation and attendance at religious services.[21] He discovered that 1 in 3 Canadian young adults who attended weekly services continue to do so today. He then made the distinction between affiliation and practice. Affiliation, he says, "is the bottom rung" of the ladder. It is identification without participation. There are many who admit to being affiliated with a faith community, but may not practise their faith. Identification is needed, however, because it may lead to attendance and participation. Those who participated in his study shared their worldviews and experience of church life. They described the world as a "place of radical instability." This instability "extends into their experience of church life." The good news is that church participation can alleviate some of the craving for calm that young Christians may experience. Hiemstra concludes that faith experience and church membership can build stability, identity and security.

Today, new expressions of Global Christianity are coming from Africa and Asia. Energy and growth are invigorating the Catholic communities in these areas. It is believed, however, that this growth is due to increases in overall population rather than conversions.[22] Looking at comparative numbers, Christianity is still the world's largest faith tradition, with 32.9% of the world's population, of which half are Catholic. Kim Cain, the communications secretary for the Global Christian Forum, indicated new developments in the area of mission, especially the New Evangelization that is the focus for Catholic and Orthodox Christians. While all Christian communities are targeted for the New Evangelization, one in particular has been the focus of much conversation: Latin America.

Another realignment has been detected in Latin America, home to half of the world's Catholics. In an interview with the *National Catholic Reporter*, Evangelical scholar William Taylor tells John Allen Jr. that "Latin American Protestants shot up from 50,000 in 1900 to 64 million in 2000, with Pentecostal and charismatic churches making up three-quarters of this number." The percentage of Protestants who make up the Latin American population has increased from 1% in 1930 to 12 to 15% today. The federation of Latin American Bishops' Conferences commissioned a study in the late 1990s that found that 8,000 Latin American Catholics were deserting the Catholic Church for Evangelical traditions every day. While this study shows how many Catholics left the tradition in the 1990s, it is difficult to know statistics on retention. Of those who leave, it is not clear how many stay with Evangelical Protestantism.

In an address to Colombian bishops, Pope Benedict XVI suggested that Catholics are converting to other Christian traditions due to a lack of fervour, joy and community in the Catholicism they experience. This means they are not converting due to doctrinal reasons:

> Growing religious pluralism is a factor that calls for serious consideration. The ever more active presence of Pentecostal and Evangelical communities, not only in Colombia, but also in many regions of Latin America, cannot be ignored or underestimated. In this connection, it is evident that the people of God are called to purify themselves and to revitalize their faith, allowing themselves to be guided by the Holy Spirit, to thus give new thrust to your pastoral action, as "many times

sincere people who leave our Church do not do so because of what 'non-Catholic' groups believe but, fundamentally, because of what they live; not for doctrinal but for existential reasons; not for strictly dogmatic but for pastoral reasons; not because of theological but methodological problems of our Church" (5th General Conference of the Latin American and Caribbean Episcopate, *Conclusive Document,* n. 225). Hence, it is about being better believers, more pious, affable and welcoming in our parishes and communities, so that no one will feel distant or excluded. Catechesis must be promoted, giving special attention to young people and adults; homilies must be carefully prepared, as well as promoting the teaching of Catholic doctrine in schools and universities. And all this to recover in the baptized a sense of belonging to the Church and to awaken in them the aspiration to share with others the joy of following Christ and of being members of his Mystical Body.[23]

Pope Benedict XVI mentions the need to be more "affable and welcoming" in our approach to evangelization. People are drawn to joy and enthusiasm and a sense of belonging. Catholics may be leaving a tradition they do not really know for the enthusiasm they find in other communities. He concludes that they may be leaving for "existential" or "pastoral" reasons.

> "And they devoted themselves to the Apostles' teaching and fellowship, to the breaking of bread and the prayers ... And day by day, attending the temple together and breaking bread in their homes, they partook of food with glad and generous hearts and praising God and having favour with all the people. And the Lord added to their number day by day those who were being saved." ꙩ ACTS 2:42, 46-47

"The Acts of the Apostles illustrates that a person cannot convey what is not believed or lived" (IL, n. 91). While the above passage from Acts refers to edible food, it also refers to the breaking of bread and prayers. These early Christians were fed by material and spiritual blessings. Their "glad and generous" hearts, coupled with their desire to praise God, demonstrate that they were well fed with the Word of God and the Bread of Life. Proper feeding led to the Lord adding "to their number day by day those who were being saved" (Acts 2:47). Here we see an example of the spiritual fruit of joy coming as a result of proper nurturing and fellowship. Popular preacher Joseph Prince once said that the pulpit is for "feeding, not for beating." Later on we will examine the need to feed with sacraments as well as witness, proclamation and deed. The New Evangelization is a response to these developments.

As Cardinal, Joseph Ratzinger addressed this progressive "de-Christianization" of traditionally Christian nations and the need for "looking for new ways to bring the Gospel to all" (Address to Catechists, 2000). He noted that many people do not find the gospel in classic evangelization:

> This is what we are searching for, along with permanent and unin-terrupted evangelization and never to be interrupted evangeliza-tion, a new evangelization capable of being heard by that world that does not find access to "classic" evangelization. Everyone needs the Gospel; the Gospel is destined to all and not only to a specific circle and this is why we are obliged to look for new ways of bringing the Gospel to all. (Address to Catechists, 2000)

There is an urgent need to present the joy of the gospel in a way that is both accessible and comprehensible. Many have already noted that Pope Francis is engaging so many people, beyond the limits of Christianity, because of his style and unique way of communicat-ing. He is continuing the legacy of previous popes in addressing the reasons why the Church has lost some members to other Christian communities.

During World Youth Day celebrations in Brazil (2013), he scold-ed the Brazilian church for losing so many Catholics to evangelical congregations:

> At times we lost people because *they don't understand what we are saying*, because we have forgotten the language of simplicity and import an intellectualism foreign to our people… Without the gram-mar of simplicity, the church loses the very conditions which make it possible to fish for God in the deep waters of his mystery…

Perhaps the church appeared too weak, perhaps too distant from their needs, perhaps too poor to respond to their concerns, perhaps too cold, perhaps too caught up with itself, perhaps a prisoner of its own rigid formulas... Perhaps the world seems to have made the church a relic of the past, unfit for new questions. Perhaps the church could speak to people in their infancy but not to those come of age. (Address to Brazilian Clergy, World Youth Day, 2013; emphasis mine).

In his first apostolic exhortation, *Evangelii Gaudium* (2013), Pope Francis argues that language that is inaccessible prevents people from accessing the "meaning, beauty and attractiveness" of the gospel (n. 34). The ability to switch gears in teaching and preaching is a necessity. At times we present the gospel in a language foreign to many. There is a need for "conversational" Church teaching. Let us see how popes have tackled the need for an evangelization that is "new."

Papal Teaching on the New Evangelization

Pope Paul VI: All Are Called to Evangelize

Evangelization "is the basic duty of the People of God."

∞ POPE PAUL VI, *EVANGELII NUNTIANDI*, N. 59

It is impossible to talk about the New Evangelization without referring to the teaching of Pope Paul VI. A year after the 3rd General Assembly of the Synod of Bishops gathered to study and reflect on evangelization, and ten years after the close of the Second Vatican Council, Pope Paul VI published his apostolic exhortation *Evangelii Nuntiandi* (Evangelization in the Modern World) on December 8, 1975. He opens with a reminder that the call to evangelize is a duty: "The preaching of the gospel to the men of our times, full as they are of hope, but harassed by fear and anxiety, must undoubtedly be regarded as a duty which will redound to the benefit, not only of the Christian community, but of the whole human race" (EN, n. 1). Evangelizing, he says, means bringing the Good News to all people. The influence of the gospel will transform "humanity from within … making it new" (EN, n. 18). Hence the need to become the best version of ourselves. All of humanity is restored and made new in Jesus Christ. The strength of the gospel can penetrate hearts and renew the face of the earth.

Interior transformation is the aim of evangelization (EN, n. 28). This transformation, however, involves the liberation that can come only with salvation in Christ (EN, n. 34). Pope Paul VI, like Pope John Paul II, taught that salvation involved liberation from radical evil. This liberation from all that enslaves us is part of what it means to be saved. The Church, teaches Paul VI, "declares that her advocacy of liberation would not be complete or perfect if she failed to preach salvation in Jesus Christ" (EN, n. 34). In other words, one cannot preach the need for liberation without the need for salvation in Jesus Christ. Authentic freedom is found in Christ. This is why the Church exists – in order to evangelize (EN, n. 14).

Earlier in the book, we explored the various levels of evangelization that Paul VI addressed. He distinguished between those who do not know Christ, those who should know Christ, and those who know him and need to deepen their faith. He provided much of the foundation for our understanding of the New Evangelization. While he was not the first to use the term "the new evangelization," the insights found in *Evangelii Nuntiandi* inspired the Latin American Bishops to use this term in 1979. Paul VI did, however, refer to new energy and enthusiasm, as well as to new methods of evangelization, as early as 1973. In *Evangelii Nuntiandi*, he refers to "a new and more fruitful era of evangelization" (n. 2). He reminded Christians that salvation is the message of evangelization. Jesus Christ became man, died and rose again in order to communicate this great gift (EN, n. 27). Jesus showed us the way to the Father and the way to restoration. An encounter with him gives us a "new nature" and reconciles us to God (EN, n. 2). The New Evangelization reproposes salvation as the "new nature" of humanity. The thought of Pope Paul VI went on to be developed by future popes and bishops.

Pope John Paul II: Do Not Be Afraid!

According to Cardinal Wuerl , "Blessed John Paul II can rightfully be considered the father of the New Evangelization."[24] John Paul II's vision of evangelization is rooted in fearlessness.

"For if I preach the Gospel, that gives me no ground for boasting. For necessity is laid upon me. Woe to me if I do not preach the Gospel."
∾ 1 CORINTHIANS 9:16

In 1973, Cardinal Karol Wojtyla celebrated an open-air Mass on Christmas night in Nowa Huta, Poland. Many were concerned that the authorities would disrupt this celebration. Many people showed up, inspiring the authorities to allow the celebration to continue uninterrupted. Cardinal Wojtyla told the crowd to not be afraid. The Communist regime was planning to build a complex that would not leave room for a church to meet the spiritual needs of the community. He encouraged members of the crowd to conquer their fear, and the celebration continued unperturbed.

Several months after the Puebla meeting of Latin American bishops in 1979, in which they used the expression "the new evangelization," Pope John Paul II returned to Poland, his homeland, in June. In his homily in Nowa Huta, he recalled the 1973 open-air Mass and, for the first time in his papacy, referred to the new evangelization:

> Wherever the cross is raised up, there arises the sign that the Good News of the salvation of man through Love has already reached that place. Wherever the cross is raised up, there is the sign that evangelization has begun. Long ago our fathers raised up the cross, in various parts of the land of Poland, as a sign that already the Gospel had arrived, that that evangelization had begun which was to be extended without interruption up to our days. With this thought in mind, the first cross was also raised in Mogila, close to Cracow, close to Stara Huta. The new cross of wood was raised up not far from here, during the celebration of the millennium. With that cross we received a sign, that is to say that on the threshold of the new millennium, in these new times, in these new conditions of life, the Gospel is proclaimed once more. A *new evangelization* has begun, as if it were a question of a second proclamation, even though in reality it is always the same. The cross stands aloft above the world as it turns on its axis.

He went on to use the expression "new evangelization" many times, in different places and on different occasions. In 1983, in an address to Latin American bishops in Haiti, he reaffirmed the vision of Paul VI by reminding the Church that the evangelizing mission of the Church is to be new in ardour, methods and expressions. In his Post-Synodal Apostolic Exhortation *Ecclesia in America* (1999), he continues to develop his thoughts on the new evangelization (n. 66). He reminds the bishops of the Americas that Christ can be encountered in the Church through scripture, liturgy and the eucharist (n. 12). Evangelization in the Americas, he says, needs to respond to the cultural demands of the context.

In *Redemptoris Missio*, his encyclical "On the Permanent Validity of the Church's Missionary Mandate" (1990), John Paul II marks the 25-year anniversary of *Ad Gentes* and the contributions Paul VI made in the area of evangelization:

> Twenty-five years after the conclusion of the Council and the publication of the Decree on Missionary Activity *Ad Gentes*, fifteen years after the Apostolic Exhortation *Evangelii Nuntiandi* issued by Pope Paul VI, and in continuity with the magisterial teaching of my predecessors, I wish to invite the Church to *renew her missionary commitment*. The present document has as its goal an interior renewal of faith and Christian life. For missionary activity renews the Church, revitalizes faith and Christian identity, and offers fresh enthusiasm and new incentive. *Faith is strengthened when it is given to others!* It is in commitment to the Church's universal mission that the new evangelization of Christian peoples will find inspiration and support. (RM, n. 2)

John Paul II emphasizes the need for evangelization because of the Church's missionary nature. He affirms the need to communicate these two truths: Jesus is the only saviour, and the Church is the universal sacrament of salvation. God desires that all people be saved and offers the Church as a sign and instrument of salvation (RM, n. 9). As the Body of Christ, our lives, the use of our gifts, and our faith are all to be signs of a grace-filled life, the result of an encounter with Christ. He goes on to emphasize the necessity of the mission *ad gentes* – in other words, to those who do not know Christ –and the mission to the baptized, a conversion of the baptized, if you will.

> "... the moment has come to commit all of the church's energies to a new evangelization and to the mission *ad gentes*. No believer in Christ, no institution of the Church can avoid this supreme duty: to proclaim Christ to all peoples." ☙ *REDEMPTORIS MISSIO*, N. 3

In his apostolic letter *Novo Millenio Ineunte* (January 6, 2001), John Paul II says that there is no time to wait; the call to evangelize is urgent. The work of evangelization is a priority for the Church because "the reality of a 'Christian society' which, amid all the frailties which have always marked human life, measured itself on Gospel values, is now gone" (n. 40). He encourages us to recall the ardour of the early Christians following the event of Pentecost. They preached, he says, with great enthusiasm and joy. In 2003, in his apostolic exhortation *Ecclesia in Europa,* he laments the "dimming of hope" and the "loss of Europe's Christian memory and heritage" (n. 7). The joy of faith has been supplanted by a kind of "practical agnosticism and religious indifference" (n. 7). European Christians, he observes, live as though they have no spiritual roots. Fear for the future has frustrated the mind and hearts of Christians. While Catholicism in Latin America has suffered due to the loss of sheep to Evangelical Protestantism, Catholicism in Europe is being strangled by "practical agnosticism and indifference."

Christ, he says, offers hope and restoration. He admits that Catholics cannot work on this life project alone; they need to be connected to other Christians. He refers to a type of ecumenical cooperation: "The future of evangelization is closely linked to the witness of unity given by all Christ's followers," (n. 54). Christ's prayer that "all may be one" (John 17:11) weaves through much of John Paul's thought.

Christian unity was also addressed by Pope Paul VI in his discussion of a new era of evangelization. Evangelization includes and involves Christians of all traditions. Throughout his papacy, John Paul II repeated the summons to the New Evangelization. He reminded all people that in Christ there is joy and relevance. We find our meaning in Christ.

Pope Benedict XVI: Rediscover the Joy

In October 2010, Pope Benedict XVI announced a new Pontifical Council for Promoting the New Evangelization. While the Pontifical Council is new, the seeds were planted at the Second Vatican Council and promoted through papal teaching and the existing Congregation for the Evangelization of Peoples. The New Evangelization, as we have seen, sets out to combat the "de-christianization" of countries that were first evangelized.[25]

> The origin of the idea can be traced back to the Second Vatican Council and its desire to respond to a sense of disorientation experienced by Christians facing powerful changes and divisions which the world was experiencing at that time. The Church's response was not characterized by pessimism or resignation (GS 1), but by the regenerating power of the universal call to salvation (LG 2), desired by God for each individual. (*Instrumentum Laboris*, n. 10).

This Pontifical Council for the Promotion of the New Evangelization now oversees both the New Evangelization and catechesis. Up until this point, guidelines for catechesis were overseen by the Congregation for the Clergy. Pope Benedict XVI outlined the specific tasks of this new council in 2010[26]:

1. To examine the theological and pastoral meaning of the New Evangelization.

2. To encourage bishops' conferences to make available magisterial teaching on the New Evangelization.

3. To make known existing projects used to promote the New Evangelization in various communities and to promote the creation of new projects.

4. To encourage the use of modern communications to promote the New Evangelization.

5. To promote the use of the *Catechism of the Catholic Church* to hand on the Catholic faith.

These developments inspired the call for a synod. On June 28, 2012, the eve of the feast of Saints Peter and Paul, at the Basilica of St. Paul Outside the Walls in Rome, Pope Benedict XVI summoned the Church to consider the task of the New Evangelization.

> "A synod is a gathering of bishops who are representative of the Church throughout the entire world. The pope convokes such a meeting, and conferences of bishops around the world elect those bishops who will attend. The pope also appoints a certain number of additional bishops, experts, and observers." ∾ CARDINAL DONALD WUERL, *NEW EVANGELIZATION: PASSING ON THE CATHOLIC FAITH TODAY*, P. 11

In his homily on that day, Pope Benedict entrusted the synod with the task of establishing new ways of re-proposing "the perennial truth of Christ's Gospel." The 13th Ordinary General Assembly of the Synod of Bishops gathered in Rome from October 7 to 28, 2012. The synod addressed "The New Evangelization for the Transmission of the Christian Faith." Apart from synod hall discussions, other documents were submitted to the synod members[27]:

- *Lineamenta* (outline of proposed document)

- *Instrumentum Laboris* (working document)

- *Relatio ante disceptationem* (report before discussion)

- *Relatio post disceptationem* (report after discussion)

At the close of the synod, Pope Benedict XVI addressed the need for pastoral ministry to be inspired and animated by the Holy Spirit; the need to reach out to those who do not know Christ and to proclaim the gospel to them; and the need to re-propose the gospel to the baptized who have fallen away from the Church for one reason or another. The Holy Press Office, with the permission of Pope Benedict XVI, released an unofficial English translation of the original Latin document containing the 58 propositions put forward by the synod fathers.[28] Cardinal Donald Wuerl, Relator of the Synod of Bishops on the New Evangelization, shares that of the 58 propositions, "all of them received nearly unanimous approbation" (Wuerl, 14). The synod fathers "have given a certain importance" to these propositions and submitted them to Pope Benedict, who then passed them on to Pope Francis, who in 2013 produced a post-synodal apostolic exhortation, *Evangelii Gaudium,* an instruction on the New Evangelization based on the propositions, working documents, and synod hall discussions. All of this took place in continuity with the Church's tradition.

The following are a few examples of the propositions put forward:[29]

• Proposition 55: Courtyard of the Gentiles

On March 25, 2011 in Paris, Pope Benedict XVI launched the Vatican's "Courtyard of the Gentiles" initiative.

> "This image refers to the vast open space near the temple of Jerusalem where all those who did not share the faith of Israel could approach the temple and ask questions about religion. There they could meet the scribes, speak of faith and even pray to the unknown God."
> ∾ POPE BENEDICT XVI, ADDRESS TO COURTYARD OF THE GENTILES, MARCH 2011

Sponsored by the Pontifical Council for Culture, this initiative promotes friendly and respectful dialogue between Christians and those who do not believe in God. "The question of God is not a menace to society; it does not threaten a truly human life! The question of God must not be absent from the other great questions of our time."[30] The first session took place in Paris in March 2011, with future events planned for Quebec, Chicago and Washington.

• Proposition 49: Pastoral Dimension of the Ordained Ministry

The Synod Fathers encourage bishops and priests to know the lives of the people they serve in a more personal way ... Ongoing formation for clergy on the New Evangelization and methods for evangelization in the diocese and parish are needed in order to learn effective means to mobilize the laity to engage in the New Evangelization.[31]

• Proposition 47: Formation for Evangelizers

This Synod considers that it is necessary to establish formation cent-
ers for the New Evangelization, where lay people learn how to speak of
the person of Christ in a persuasive manner adapted to our time and to
specific groups of people (young people, agnostics, the elderly and so
forth).[32]

Both of these propositions underline the need for trained clergy,
religious and laity. While advanced studies in theology introduce one
to the language of theology, this language can be difficult for the begin-
ner. These propositions encourage training in the area of communication and overall presentation of the faith.

When Pope Benedict XVI unveiled the new Vatican agency, the
Pontifical Council for the Promotion of the New Evangelization, he
said that the new council will encourage a clear understanding of the
faith. Along with Pope Benedict, other popes – such as Pope Paul VI
and Pope Francis – have noted the need to preach the gospel in clear
and convincing ways (EN, n. 3). One of the problems noted during the
First Evangelization was the unconvincing way in which the gospel
was preached in certain contexts. Ongoing catechesis, Pope Benedict
XVI says, should make use of the *Catechism of the Catholic Church*
and other treasures of the Church. This aim was made clear when he
announced the Year of Faith. On October 17, 2011, he formally announced this special year in an apostolic letter, *Porta Fidei* ("The Door
of Faith"). The observance would begin October 11, 2012, the 50th
Anniversary of opening of the Second Vatican Council, and close on
November 23, 2013. The year was to focus on belief and evangelization.

Evangelizing hearts means re-proposing Jesus Christ as the answer
to all anguish and longing. Jesus is depending on us, the members of
his body, to reveal his glory and the power of his transforming love.
The pope reminded Catholics that passing through the door begins
with baptism and lasts a lifetime. The "door of faith" (Acts 14:27) "is
always open for us, ushering us into the life of communion with God
and offering entry into his church" (*Porta Fidei*, n. 1).

A nurtured faith life will help us recognize Christ in our neighbour. Pope Benedict's hope was that this year of faith would help Catholics appreciate the gift of faith and share that gift with others. This rediscovery of faith and joy would deepen their relationship with God and encourage them to become reacquainted with the riches of our tradition: namely, the *Catechism of the Catholic Church* and the documents of the Second Vatican Council.[33] It would seem, however, that this initiative mainly targeted Catholics who make up that second category of those in need of evangelization: those who know Christ, practise their faith, but need to deepen their commitment in order to nurture an encounter with Christ as a person. It is this group, I believe, who will evangelize the third: those who are baptized but do not practise their faith, those who have fallen away from the Church for one reason or another. The clergy, religious and laity who make up this second group will be the ones called to witness and proclamation.

Pope Francis: A Culture of Encounter

"I want to see the church get closer to the people..."
ꙮ POPE FRANCIS, JULY 25, 2013, WORLD YOUTH DAY, BRAZIL

Pope Francis has surprised many Christians with his spontaneous style and improvisational approach to preaching and teaching. In an unscripted homily given on April 28, 2013, he addressed a group of individuals receiving the sacrament of Confirmation. He inspired the crowd with his words of encouragement, telling them to "swim against the tide" and be open to the work of the Holy Spirit. He told them that the Holy Spirit brings the "new things of God" and changes us by making all things new.[34]

"The joy of the gospel fills the hearts and lives of all who encounter Jesus." ꙮ POPE FRANCIS, *EVANGELII GAUDIUM*, N. 1

In another homily, for the Mass of the feast of St. George on April 23, 2013, the pope gives courage to those who support the missionary nature of the Church. He reminds us of the courage of the first disciples, who had the daunting task of bringing the gospel to the Greeks. He refers to the Book of Acts (11:19-20) and how proclaiming Jesus to the Greeks or Gentiles was considered "scandalous," but they did it anyway. They were able to do this, he says, because they were part of the Church. We need the Church to experience Jesus:

> Unless we are "Jesus' sheep," faith does not come; it is a faith that is watered down, insubstantial. And let us think of the consolation Barnabas experienced, which was precisely the 'delightful and comforting joy of evangelizing.' Let us ask the Lord for this *parrhesia*, this apostolic fervor that impels us to move forward as brothers and sisters, all of us: forward![35]

These words can inspire us to evangelize in our own contexts. Pope Francis reminds us that the early disciples risked death and persecution in their evangelizing efforts.

In a May 8, 2013, homily, he distinguished between evangelization and proselytism. He gave the example of St. Paul, who did not proselytize, because he knew Jesus Christ. St. Paul, he says, was sure of his relationship with Jesus, so there was no need to force conversions. St. Paul had the courage to go to the outskirts of his familiar surroundings and preach the gospel. Zeal inspires, whereas use of force alienates and discourages.

Pope Francis encourages us to evangelize with "apostolic zeal." So far, his papacy has been marked with enthusiasm and encouragement. Evangelization, for him, involves building bridges, not walls. Be sure of who you are and who Christ is, and you will have the courage to bring Christ to others, even in unknown territory. He develops his thoughts on evangelization in *Evangelii Gaudium.* We will hear from this apostolic exhortation throughout this book.

John Allen Jr., an American Catholic journalist who has been reporting from the Vatican for many years, observes that Pope Francis' approach to evangelization is marked by three key themes:[36]

1. New Vision of Leadership: Evangelizers must take on "the smell of the sheep" (EG, n. 24). This includes the call for clergy to be more consultative and collaborative.

2. Social Gospel: John Allen Jr. refers to Pope Francis as the "Pope of the Poor." During World Youth Day (Brazil, 2013), Pope Francis reminded the more underprivileged participants that the "church is with you."

3. Mercy: "The salvation which God offers us is the work of his mercy" (EG, n. 112). Pope Francis reminds us that we may tire of going to God, but God never tires of forgiving us.

While he is not the first to address these themes,[37] it is clear that Pope Francis is touching many through his spontaneous approach and popular appeal. His charisma and outgoing personality have presented the never-changing truths of our tradition in a new way. Continuing the good work of his predecessors, he is a missionary pope. The following quote captures the vision of Pope Francis: "I prefer a Church which is bruised, hurting and dirty because it has been out on the streets, rather than a Church which is unhealthy from being confined and from clinging to its own security" (EG, n. 49).

5

Witness and Proclamation: Seeing Salvation

"Master, now you are dismissing your servant in peace, according to your word; **for my eyes have seen your salvation**, which you have prepared in the presence of all peoples, a light for revelation to the Gentiles and for glory to your people Israel." ∾ LUKE 2:29-32, THE WORDS OF SIMEON AT THE PRESENTATION OF JESUS

Witness

Our tradition has affirmed over and over again that the first form of evangelization is witness.[38] Witness refers to witnessing something, hearing something, or experiencing something. While proclamation has to do with speaking, a public announcement of sorts, witness does not involve speaking. Webster's dictionary defines witness as "A person who has seen, experienced, or heard something; something serving as proof or evidence." In other words, to be a witness to Christ, or to witness, you must have experienced an encounter with him. You know him and have been transformed as a result. Abraham and Paul were not converted by a written text – they were converted through an encounter with God. Preaching and teaching involve going out and using words to communicate something about Christ; witness, on the other hand, is needed *before* words. It involves the overall presence of a person serving as a sign: love evangelizes and transforms.

> "Modern man listens more willingly to witnesses than to teachers, and if he does listen to teachers, it is because they are witnesses ... It is therefore primarily by her conduct and by her life that the Church will evangelize the world, in other words, by her living witness of fidelity to the Lord Jesus, by her witness of poverty and detachment, and by her witness of freedom in the face of the powers of this world, in short the witness of sanctity." ∾ POPE PAUL VI, *EVANGELII NUNTIANDI*, N. 41

Paul VI referred to a "silent witness" of spiritual poverty, detachment from material things, chastity, love of neighbour, and challenging others to revisit their actions and thoughts through the silent witness of their own lives. This silent witness, he says, is a form of preaching (EN, n. 69). Witnessing to the gospel through your personal and social life is powerful. An evangelist will witness with the beauty of his or her life lived in the gospel message. The words follow, and hopefully they will be the fruit of inner transformation.

The *Decree on Missionary Activity* (n. 40) affirmed that the person who evangelizes must be himself evangelized and converted. What is needed is consistency between what a person says and what she does. Recall the meaning of Jesus' name: God's salvation. When Mary and Joseph brought Jesus to the temple, the prophet Simeon says, "…my eyes have seen your salvation" (see Luke 2:21-38). Salvation, as we saw earlier, is the restoration of the image and likeness of God. Jesus reveals these mysteries to us: who God is and who we are called to be, fully restored. We gain divine health after an encounter with him. Simeon and others who walked with Jesus sensed this mystery.

We are called to bring Christ to others so that they will sense his presence in us; others will see salvation in us. It is the Holy Spirit who brings this about. As Pope Paul VI said, "there can be no evangelization without the cooperation of the Holy Spirit" (EN, n. 75). A lifetime of prayer, humility, love and patience bears great fruit and is visible. Others will notice a difference and will see the process of salvation unfolding before their very eyes. A person who had been cranky and impatient becomes thoughtful and caring. Our transformation communicates the good news of Jesus Christ.

People need witnesses because they need to see salvation like Simeon did. How do we know we are in the presence of someone on the way to being restored? We are fed by her presence. Her presence restores, brings joy and satisfaction. The words are important and will have a role to play later, but for now people need to see it lived, so that the words will inform their faith journey. We are the Body of Christ and need to act like it. Father Robert Barron, in an address to seminarians, expressed the need for great evangelizers to be in love with Jesus Christ.[39] When someone falls in love, meets a terrific friend, watches a moving play, or discovers a beautiful piece of music, there is a desire to share this beauty with others, to pass it on. Others notice the joy in the person's faces as he or she shares this good news, because they can see it.

> "You will be my witnesses in Jerusalem, and in all Judea and Samaria, and to the ends of the earth." ∽ ACTS 1:8B

Some people will be more moved by seeing the good news in people, while others can manage with words and other types of formation. Proclamation alone does not bring everyone to Christ. Joseph Ratzinger, in his address to catechists, warned that we must make the Church's teaching more accessible and comprehensible. Our presentation of the faith must be clear and convincing. Not everyone is fed by reading official documents or the lives of the saints. Some people need to witness what an encounter with Christ achieves in one's life journey.

For many years, friends have commented on how often I wear black: black skirts, black sweaters, black pants, etc. Some have tried to psychoanalyze me over and over again: "She's trying to make a statement about how she's feeling. She's very mysterious, that's why she wears black." Lately, it's been "Is it part of the dress code at the seminary? Does everyone wear black?" Eventually, it was my husband who solved the mystery. One day he said, "Could it be you wear black all the time because you don't know how to put clothes together?" Bingo! He was right! I do not know how to match patterns and colours. To be honest, it drives me crazy. There are many men and women who can go into a department store and mix and match and put an outfit together. I need mannequins, and lots of them. I need to see how someone else put together an outfit. If I see an outfit put together, I am more likely to buy it.

Just as I need to see an outfit put together in order to invest in it, some people need to see what salvation looks like. While some may be able to navigate through this great church, finding the Catechism, joining a prayer group, taking courses in bible study, and so on, these are the people who know how it all fits together. Others do not know where to start. They need to see your faith in action: wearing the ashes on your forehead to the grocery store on Ash Wednesday; blessing yourself before a meal in a restaurant, working in a food bank. You are the billboard for the message of the New Evangelization: salvation. Your life, actions and words are the message! Do others see salvation in you? Once someone sees how your faith life has made you more joyful, patient, loving and resilient, they may be open to finding out more about this "secret" of yours.

"Today's world is one that is constantly bombarded with words and information. For this reason and possibly more than at any time in recent history, the things Christians do speak louder than the things they say." ∾ JOHN PAUL II, ADDRESS TO THE BISHOPS OF THE PHILIPPINES, OCTOBER 30, 2003

Patricia Treece, in her book *The Sanctified Body*,[40] has looked into this "secret" of sanctity. She spent many years studying the lives of the saints and the records of interviews conducted with those who witnessed their sanctity. Apart from studying the physiology of sanctity (such as luminosity and perfumes of sanctity), she discovered that people of sanctity, holy and whole people, shared the following virtues:

• Large-mindedness

- Optimism

- Realism

- Inner joy

- Steady good-naturedness

- Spiritual wisdom

- Simplicity

- Strong sense of humour

- Great humility

These qualities can speak louder than words because they are the fruit of a lifelong journey of hope and transformation. How did they get there? Who witnessed to them? When did proclamation enter the picture? Don Everts and Doug Schaupp spent ten years doing qualitative research studying the conversion of skeptics.[41] These researchers remind us not to use a "cookie cutter" approach to evangelization. Each person is unique, with his or her own learning style, family of origin, joys and sorrows, education, work experience and personality type. An approach that works for me may not work for another person who is searching for the truth and God.

Everts and Schaupp discovered five important shifts that one experiences on the way to conversion. I will list them and use them as a framework as I add my own commentary as it applies to the Catholic tradition. The stages or thresholds through which people pass represent the journey from witness to proclamation.

TRANSITIONING FROM WITNESS TO PROCLAMATION: REACHING THOSE WHO HAVE FALLEN AWAY FROM THE CHURCH

1. From distrust to trust

Dr. James Fowler, in his research on faith development,[42] tells us that at some point in a person's life, as they are still immature in their faith journey, they may equate their image of God or the church with a person in a position of authority. The good news is that if the person of authority is kind and life-giving, this may be a positive influence, as this person can be used as an instrument to bring another to God and back to the church. As the person's faith life matures, they will discover that God is not limited to people or institutions. God used the person of faith to communicate God's love and wisdom. The bad news is that a person in a position of authority may use this position to manipulate and hurt others. If those in his care have projected his image onto the whole Church, this is dangerous, and faith is at risk of being lost. Certainly the recent sexual abuse scandals in the Church have hurt many victims and their loved ones. These victims may feel disillusioned and betrayed, and they may distrust the whole community of faith. This may lead to a worst-case scenario: their image of God may be destroyed.

Everts and Schaupp give us some examples of individuals who did not trust the Church because of their interactions with people or media who are not life-giving and do not present an authentic picture of the faith: "Christa doesn't trust Christians because she was once told she's going straight to hell. A professor told Ryan that the Bible is full of mistakes. Bonnie read *The Da Vinci Code* and thinks the church is one big conspiracy. Julie was invited to a church outing but felt like an outsider the entire time."[43] These people need to trust another Christian who reveals Christ and his goodness, which may involve a lengthy process and heroic patience. They need to see salvation at work, in the family, in the parish and in all sectors of society.

On the other hand, someone who has fallen away from the Church may need a powerful witness in order to woo them back. I know a person who experienced a great spark of interest in Catholicism and God due to the homily preached by a priest at her friend's wedding. This person is now a tremendous leader in the Catholic Church. It was not just the words of the homily; it was the priest's overall presence and joy. He was kind and welcoming, putting everyone at ease with his humour and hospitality. She began to worship on a regular basis, and her trust in this priest led to a fruitful prayer life.

If someone does not trust God, we owe it to her to discover why. The very first time we are called to trust God is the most difficult. Here are a few examples of situations that may challenge us to trust God:

- The death of a loved one

- Separation or divorce

- A newly diagnosed illness

- Conflict in the workplace or in the family

- Job loss

- Poverty

- A daunting task

While the outcome may not be what we expected, we may discover a newfound resiliency, strength and joy when we realized that God's faithfulness helped us survive the struggle. God shows us his support and love through the love of friends and family: friends drop off food after the death of a loved one; family members offer to pick up the kids from school while you are off sick; someone buys you an inspirational book to lift your spirits after a job loss. We learn to trust through God's faithfulness and goodness through the witness of others. This trust may lead some to ask questions about their faith. In his encyclical *Deus Caritas Est* (God is love), Pope Benedict XVI says that it is best for Christians to know "when it is time to speak of God and when it is better to say nothing and let love alone speak" (n. 31c). Love heals and restores and will inspire curiosity. The pastoral care of people is part of the Church's evangelizing mission (EG, n. 14).

2. From complacency to curiosity

In their study, Everts and Schaupp warn that curiosity does not mean conversion. Once you are trusted as a Christian, someone may look to you as an authority figure. Do not worry that you don't know all of the answers, as long as you know where to look, who to ask, which books to recommend. My daughter's dance teacher noticed the ashes on my forehead on Ash Wednesday; this led to a wonderful discussion about Christianity. Our painter watched a movie on YouTube that challenged the historical existence of Jesus Christ. He asked me if the documentary was right in declaring that Jesus never existed, that he was a composite of a variety of mythological deities. Luckily, as a theologian who teaches Christology, I was able to respond and tell him that apart from the scriptures, there are pagan and Jewish historians dating back to the first centuries of Christianity who have documented the historical reality of Jesus. Moreover, there is art from the first centuries depicting Jesus as a young man, without a beard, healing people, eating with them, and raising Lazarus from the dead. The painter was delighted to hear these details about proofs validating the life of Jesus, as he was concerned about the impact this video was having on those whose faith is fragile.

> "You may be the only Gospel your neighbour ever meets."
> ∾ CANADIAN CONFERENCE OF CATHOLIC BISHOPS, *ON GOOD SOIL*, P. 69

3. From closed to change to open to change

Some people may be afraid to take it to this level, as they fear that conversion means they will be crucified, that practising one's faith means lack of freedom, that it involves rules and regulations, and no joy. They are worried about what they will have to give up and how their lives will no longer be the same.

Hopefully, someone in this stage will discover that openness to change means openness to restoration and transformation. If we lose something, such as harshness, sarcasm, the tendency to gossip or lie, or jealousy, we did not need it in the first place. The mystics tell us that souls go through three stages: purgative, illuminative, and unitive.[44] In a nutshell, this means that once you turn your life over to God and his plan, God begins to weed out all habits, thoughts and speech that are not life-giving. While it may be difficult to give up what is familiar, the purification is really restoration. God is in the restoration business, not the destruction business.

Slowly and according to God's timing, God reveals to us those parts of ourselves that are not bearing fruit, those parts of ourselves that tear others down, that lead to self-loathing. I refer to these purifying moments as *purgatorial pinches*. These spiritual pinches are reminders of those moments where we failed to be life-giving through our action or inaction. Humility and self-awareness are key to understanding the spiritual journey. When we are humble enough to know ourselves – "What does it feel like to be in my presence?" – we know how to pray: Lord, help me with my impatience, Lord, deliver me from this habit, and so on. It may even lead to seeing ourselves the way others see us, the way the Lord sees us.

There is an interesting video on YouTube produced by Dove, the makers of soap and other related products. It is called Dove Sketches. In the video, a forensic artist is asked to draw two separate images of women: one based on a woman's self-perception, how she sees herself, and another based on the information collected from a person who has met her and has enough memory of this encounter to describe her to the artist. The key is that the women being described in the images do not face the artist. He does not see her face to face; he has to go by her description of herself. It was surprising to see how different the images were; those based on the object's self-disclosure were harsher and tended to exaggerate certain perceived flaws. In the portraits based on their own self-understanding, the women appeared older and more tired. The images based on the witness of the other participants were softer, and more closely resembled the women they represented; they were closest to the real person. It was clear from this video that there are women who perceive themselves more negatively than others perceive them.

We can be sure that there are people who do not perceive themselves the way God sees them: as his cherished child. Once our sense of self is healed with the acceptance of God's love and self-knowledge, the journey begins to take off. We need love of self, love of others, and God's love. We cannot fully and unconditionally love other people if we do not love ourselves. If we see only the flaws and mistakes, we will compare ourselves to others, which leads to jealousy, envy and judgment. Love of self does not mean passivity or self-centredness; it means a humble openness to change that does not lead to self-loathing. We enter the illuminative stage where we begin to see our life in a new light. The light of Christ reveals the truth of every situation.

The other day my husband and I were sitting enjoying our morning coffee. Rays of sunshine came beaming through our kitchen window. As beautiful as this glorious natural light was, it showed all the areas of the kitchen that required a thorough cleaning, namely the stainless steel exterior of my stove! At first I thought, maybe Rob won't notice it. But sure enough, Rob said, "Look at that stove!" We both agreed that it needed cleaning. While the natural light of the sun warmed our hearts that day, it revealed the dirt. In this illuminative stage, the believer continues to learn and grow, to see the truth, but always with the warmth of God's love and tenderness. God's love sheds light on all aspects of our lives. God knows our stamina and will reveal those areas in need of purification in stages we can endure. We receive these insights and the healing that follows in manageable installments. Certain dark areas are uncovered in doses so that they are manageable, and all the while we know we are loved and not abandoned. God does this not to punish, but to heal and restore.

You may find yourself going back and forth between the first two stages: purification followed by illumination, then back to another area in need of purification, then illumination. This requires courage and trust. Some may say, "I like Jesus, but am I ready to change?" The encounter with Christ does leave us changed; we evaluate how we have been satisfying our thirst elsewhere, only to be disappointed or frustrated because the thirst remains. The married woman who has been having lunch with a co-worker about whom she daydreams, and with whom she flirts, will have to rein it in and draw closer to her husband; the man who is stealing from work will have to stop and restore that which has been taken; the teenager who is slandering friends online will have to stop, apologize and restore the reputations that have been destroyed. The man who abuses his wife or child will have to respond to offers of therapy and discover the fear, self-loathing, woundedness and projection that may have led to the abusive behaviour. The woman who lied and cheated her way all the way to the top of the corporate ladder will have to examine her conscience and the hurt she caused others.

The path may be challenging, but the rewards are priceless, including a new life rooted in authentic freedom. The former drug dealer who loathes himself and feels unworthy of a new life and forgiveness will realize that God's love and mercy are greater than his own greatest sin. The "god" he made of his wound will be destroyed and his sense of self will be healed. Change is all about healing and being fed. It is the work of the Holy Spirit that brings this change about. We will be saying to one another, "Hey, I love what the Holy Spirit is doing with you!" The language of the Holy Spirit is truth, and its power is the love of God. Truth and the love of God can transform us from within, but we need to be open to healing. The need for change and reconciliation inspired Cardinal Timothy Dolan, archbishop of New York, to recommend to the Synod on the New Evangelization that the sacrament of reconciliation be considered the "sacrament of the New Evangelization."[45] This sacrament brings healing and growth and the courage to face the future with hope. What we perceive as the demanding side of evangelization is really the healing and restoration God offers. After the pain of the cross comes the joy of the resurrection, where pain and sorrow are redeemed. A new life is possible. The witness of this transformation in others is remarkable. One of my students, Trevor, once said, "You cannot argue with witness." You cannot argue with transformation; this speaks for itself. Finally, we come to the unitive stage, where union with God brings much satisfaction. The next thresholds show the way to this final stage.

> "What the world is in particular need of today is the credible witness of people enlightened in mind and heart by the word of the Lord, and capable of opening the hearts and minds of many to the desire for God and for true life, life without end." ∾ POPE BENEDICT XVI, *PORTA FIDEI*, N. 15

4. Seeking God's will

By this point, we come to trust God's will and plan. There is a sense that God's plan is all about authentic freedom and protection. Adam and Eve did not trust the plan. They felt limited by it; they did not believe that it was put in place so they could be really free and protected at the same time. This lack of trust, this impatience and inability to accept their limitations as creatures, led them to think they could be like God without obeying God. In this stage, we trust God's plan and grow in spiritual stamina and endurance, like the athlete St. Paul talks about. In seasons of plenty, when life is good and all is flourishing, we pray in gratitude and continue to pray for self-knowledge and conversion so that when the seasons of drought come, sometimes overnight, where there is "weeping and gnashing of teeth" (Luke 13:28), suffering, unemployment and loss, we have the stamina to experience "the peace that surpasses all understanding" (Philippians 4:7). Seeking the will of God is a sign of spiritual maturity.[46] Trusting God's will and being patient with his plan leads to restoration and flourishing. Impatience, distrust and restlessness may lead to our own woundedness and the woundedness of others. Writer Hal Borland once wrote, "God's delays are not God's denials." Trusting in God's will requires patience and prayer for inner peace. A delay may mean God has something else in mind, or the answer may be a no, requiring heroic trust.

5. Entering the Kingdom of God

In Christian theology, we speak of an "already, but not yet" when it comes to experiencing the fullness of God's kingdom. Jesus, in the Lord's Prayer, includes the petition asking for God's kingdom to come. Jesus goes on to teach that the kingdom of God is like a mustard seed. The seed needs to be fed with love, humility, trust, detachment and the pursuit of truth. The more people become another Christ, those in whom others see salvation, the more others experience the kingdom of God. However, sin persists as some people continue to distrust God, act impulsively, lack self-knowledge, and work out the plan for their lives with impatience and lack of reason and trust; the kingdom is not yet fully experienced. Those who are seeking and open to conversion need continual nourishment. They have passed through the need for witness, and now they need to be fed with the sacraments and the written and spoken word.

70

Proclamation

> "... this announcing of Christ by a living testimony as well as by the spoken word takes on a specific quality and a special force in that it is carried out in the ordinary surroundings of the world."
>
> ᗩ *LUMEN GENTIUM*, N. 35

A proclamation is a form of public announcement. As Christians, we announce the good news of Jesus Christ using words in preaching, teaching and writing. Jesus is risen! Jesus is the Son of God, the Messiah, one with God and one with us!

We can experience the power of the resurrection in our own lives and become a new creation. The same power that brought this about in Christ will make us new: "If the Spirit of him who raised Jesus from the dead dwells in you, he who raised Christ from the dead will give life to your mortal bodies also through this spirit that dwells in you" (Romans 8:11). Note that St. Paul refers to the present: "your mortal bodies," suggesting that new life can begin in this lifetime. Sorrow can be redeemed; bad habits can be conquered; the correction of perception can renew our minds so that we can put on "the mind of Christ" (1 Corinthians 2:16). This good news is to be communicated in homilies, teaching and reflections, using the written word and media and social communications.[47]

> "... they whose function it is to proclaim the Word must exercise every care to ensure that their words are dignified, well chosen and adapted to their audience." ᗩ POPE PAUL VI, *EVANGELII NUNTIANDI*, N. 73

In his book *Why Preach? Encountering Christ in God's Word*, Father Peter John Cameron refers to *preaching as an encounter*.[48] Those who are fed by the word use this nourishment to inspire an encounter with Christ. Those who preach share their own encounter with the Lord as they break open the word for us. Father Cameron asserts that this process of encounter begins with human experience.

My husband reminds me on a regular basis to include stories in my writing and public speaking. People relate to human experience and our own encounter with the Lord through our heartache and celebration. Someone once asked me for a biography to use in her introduction of me for a talk I would be facilitating. She wanted to know a little about me so she could give the audience a sense of who I am. I sent her an email with some of my credentials and professional experience. She wrote back asking if I could call her about the biography. I am so glad I did, because she reminded me that people want to know the "real me" – what made me who I am and what kinds of experiences informed my faith experience. She wanted a few "lines" to give the audience an idea of who I am. She said, "I read your biography and I don't see Josie. I see Dr. Josephine Lombardi, but I do not see you as a person."

People are moved and inspired by authenticity, examples of lived faith and life experience. Mothers want to hear that there are others who relate to their sacrifices. Single people want to hear that their witness is just as powerful as that of priests or married people. People who have gone through separation or divorce want to hear that there is hope for their future. A father who has lost a child needs to hear that God is with him.

Those who are further along on the journey can use their life experience to give hope to those who find themselves carrying their own personal cross, or living through a season of drought. The widow who lost her husband 20 years ago can share that the waves and pangs of grief are not as frequent or long-lasting as they used to be. She continues to miss her husband and grieve his loss, but she is amazed that she has survived it. She went from being in the eye of the hurricane to being a category one in the hurricane of grief. The child who was told that he would not accomplish anything in life can share how his faith and the inspiration of other faith-filled people led him to pursue his dreams and conquer not only his own fears, but those projected onto him.

The hope that is the fruit of conquered sorrows feeds those who are discouraged. Human experience, the word and the sacrament feed people as they seek to become the best version of themselves. Several acquaintances have shared with me that there were times when they thought the priest was speaking directly to them. The Holy Spirit works through the preacher or teacher and can use certain opportunities to encourage and console those who need it.

"The style of evangelical preaching should have this attitude: humility, service, charity, brotherly love." ∽ POPE FRANCIS, FEAST OF ST. MARK, APRIL 25, 2013

To be sure, we are fed by the sacraments, especially the Eucharist. Jesus is the Bread of Life who feeds us in the Eucharist and in the spoken word. There is something about bread that satisfies us. Studies show that good carbohydrates help us sleep better and help stabilize moods.[49] There is a reason why Jesus said he is the bread of life, not the fish of life or the olive of life, not even the chips of life! He feeds us in a way that satisfies, giving us a foretaste of heaven. In an unpublished manuscript on purgatory, we hear heaven described this way: "Heaven is above all and beyond all – God: God loved, God relished, God delighted in; in one word, it is to be satisfied with God without ever being satisfied."[50]

We crave fulfillment and satisfaction. We crave to be fed by the spoken word. This is why some Christians flock to evangelical preachers. Skilled preachers are able to switch gears and make the gospel accessible. The use of technical, abstract language can alienate and starve a congregation. Those who have been fed and have knowledge of the richness of our tradition have the duty to share and feed others. If the tradition is not made accessible or comprehensible, we are guilty of hoarding religious truths. We need to train those who can feed others using user-friendly language. Sharing the lived experience and reality of the gospel in user-friendly language is more effective than starving people with language that is too abstract and technical. If the gospel is not connected to the personal lives of Christians, it remains distant.

"For example, if in the course of the liturgical year a parish priest speaks about temperance ten times but only mentions charity or justice two or three times, an imbalance results, and precisely those virtues which ought to be most present in preaching and catechesis are overlooked. The same thing happens when we speak more about law than about grace, more about the Church than about Christ, more about the Pope than about God's Word." ∾ POPE FRANCIS, *EVANGELII GAUDIUM*, N. 38

Accessible language is clear and convincing. Some people will pick up an encyclical, while others would rather watch a YouTube video. People of different age groups, with language barriers or learning disabilities may find it difficult to follow an overly technical homily or reflection. Over and over again in my courses in systematic theology, I encourage my students to imagine explaining the mysteries of our faith to Grade 6 students. It can be surprisingly difficult. Recall Pope Benedict's response to the challenge of losing Catholics to Evangelical Protestantism; he said that these communities are attracting our membership due to their joy and enthusiasm, not for doctrinal reasons. The ability to switch gears and proclaim the word of God using user-friendly language will make our tradition accessible and comprehensible.

"A preacher who does not prepare is not " spiritual"; he is dishonest and irresponsible with the gifts he has received." ∾ POPE FRANCIS, *EVANGELII GAUDIUM*, N. 145

Just the other day I found myself doing this in a television interview. I was talking about salvation and redemption and at one point I referred to "the Fall." I was referring to the sin of Adam and Eve, but I did not clarify. When I watched the interview I wondered how many people were thinking: "What is she talking about? Who fell and what does this have to do with salvation?" I could not retrieve that moment and I may have lost an opportunity to make Church teaching more accessible.

> "Some people think they can be good preachers because they know what ought to be said, but they pay no attention to **how** it should be said, that is, the concrete way of constructing a sermon."
> ꙮ POPE FRANCIS, *EVANGELII GAUDIUM*, N. 156

Ongoing formation for priests and deacons in the area of preaching is a must. However, one forgotten piece is that lay people are allowed to preach outside of the Eucharistic liturgy. The Church allows for lay preaching in certain contexts (see Canon 766 of the New Code of Canon Law). Canon 766 is one of those canons that "conclude with a stipulation that it is to be implemented according to the prescriptions of the conference of Bishops. Each national conference of Bishops was charged with the responsibility to determine what norms of implementation would enable the emerging ministry of lay preaching to best serve their local Churches."[51] The Canadian bishops passed norms of implementation in 1985. While the Canadian bishops do not provide detailed instructions on where lay preaching is to take place, they make it clear that it is not to occur "within the celebration of the Eucharist at the moment reserved for the homily." As long as there is no confusion with the homily, it is implied that lay people can preach, facilitate conferences and offer instruction in other contexts, such as retreats, prayer services and parish missions outside of Mass. The United States Conference of Catholic Bishops issued a Decree of Promulgation in 2001 offering an instruction on Lay Preaching. I include part of it here:

Complementary Norm: Preaching the Word of God is among the principal duties of those who have received the sacrament of orders (cc. 762–764). The lay faithful can be called to cooperate in the exercise of the Ministry of the Word (c. 759). In accord with canon 766 the National Conference of Catholic Bishops hereby decrees that the lay faithful may be permitted to exercise this ministry in churches and oratories, with due regard for the following provisions: If necessity requires it in certain circumstances or it seems useful in particular cases, the diocesan bishop can admit lay faithful to preach, to offer spiritual conferences or give instructions in churches, oratories or other sacred places within his diocese, when he judges it to be to the spiritual advantage of the faithful. In order to assist the diocesan bishop in making an appropriate pastoral decision (Interdicasterial Instruction, *Ecclesiae de Mysterio*, Article 2 §3), the following circumstances and cases are illustrative: the absence or shortage of clergy, particular language requirements, or the demonstrated expertise or experience of the lay faithful concerned. The lay faithful who are to be admitted to preach in a church or oratory must be orthodox in faith, and well-qualified, both by the witness of their lives as Christians and by a preparation for preaching appropriate to the circumstances. The diocesan bishop will determine the appropriate situations in accord with canon 772, §1. In providing for preaching by the lay faithful the diocesan bishop may never dispense from the norm which reserves the homily to the sacred ministers (c. 767, §1; cfr. Pontifical Commission for the Authentic Interpretation of the Code of Canon Law, 26 May 1987, in AAS 79 [1987], 1249). Preaching by the lay faithful may not take place within the Celebration of the Eucharist at the moment reserved for the homily.

While there are restrictions placed on lay preaching, the *Directory of Masses for Children*, published by the Congregation for Divine Worship in 1973, states that "one of the adults may speak after the gospel, especially if the priest finds it hard to adapt himself to the mentality of children" (n. 24). This means there are opportunities for qualified, faith-filled lay people to preach. Bishops are encouraged to seek out such individuals and assess their qualifications and gifts. The challenge is to ensure proper training. In a course I teach at St. Augustine's Seminary, Lay Ministry in the Diocesan Church, I include a unit on lay preaching. After clarifying the Church's teaching, laws and norms regarding lay preaching, I offer a model to be used to plan and deliver a preached reflection. There are many lay people with wonderful communication skills, but they may lack proper training in theology and homiletics. It can be disastrous when someone who is not informed is entrusted with the task of forming other individuals. One person's misunderstanding can misinform others. It is best in these circumstances to admit not knowing and to take the time to get the answers from those who have the background.

While the Church is clear on its instruction for formal lay preaching, Pope Francis encourages informal lay preaching in *Evangelii Gaudium*:

> How beautiful it is to see that young people are 'street preachers', joyfully bringing Jesus to every street, every town square and every corner of the earth! (EG, n. 106)

> Today, as the Church seeks to experience a profound missionary renewal, there is a kind of preaching which falls to each of us as a daily responsibility. It has to do with bringing the Gospel to the people we meet, whether they be our neighbours or complete strangers. This is the informal preaching which takes place in the middle of a conversation, something along the lines of what a missionary does when visiting a home. Being a disciple means being constantly ready to bring the love of Jesus to others, and this can happen unexpectedly and in any place: on the street, in a city square, during work, on a journey. (EG, n. 127)

In contrast with the teaching of *Ad Gentes* (n. 40), Pope Francis goes on to say that we should not be afraid to evangelize even though we are in constant need of being evangelized ourselves: "each of us should find ways to communicate Jesus wherever we are" (EG, n. 121). As we mature in our evangelizing efforts, we deepen our love for the Lord and offer a "clearer witness to the Gospel" (EG, n. 121).

The Second Vatican Council not only affirmed the universal call to holiness regardless of state of life, it affirmed the gifts of the laity and encouraged lay people to contribute their gifts to the Church and to use their faith to evangelize in their homes and workplaces. Several official documents affirm the collaboration between clergy and laity.[52] Official Church teaching makes it clear that laypeople cannot replace clergy; we can assist in a variety of ministries, feeding people with our own life experience as mothers, fathers, husbands, wives, daughters, single people, nurses, and so on. Teachers in the classroom can use their gifts to show that they are people of faith. We must ask ourselves, "Am I making the faith attractive?" Does the witness of my life encourage another person to seek that vocation that will keep him close to God?

The bishop who confirmed my eldest daughter said in his homily at the celebration, "Jesus is both attractive and demanding." Are we projecting only the demanding side of our faith? Can others see the attractive Christ in us? As we grow to become another Christ, it is the Christ in us who woos others to him. It is his love and compassion that they sense. Our lives are joined to his; our unique personalities remain and we cooperate with his love and grace. Our lives offer a foretaste of the heavenly banquet that awaits us. We evangelize with witness and proclamation and pray for the wisdom to know the difference. It is our duty to evangelize because the Church is missionary by its very nature (EN, n. 14).

6

Areas of Our Society that Need an Encounter with Jesus Christ

"Go into all the world and proclaim the good news to the whole creation." ∽ MARK 16:15

Pope Paul VI declared that Christians are to carry forth "the good news to every sector" (*Evangelii Nuntiandi*, n. 18). It is our duty to make God known, to re-propose Christ and salvation. This encounter will transform individuals, restoring them to divine health. The fruit of this transformation will in turn spill over into the various sectors that make up our lived reality.

The working document for the synod on the New Evangelization lists seven sectors in need of an encounter with Christ:

- Culture: Encountering Christ in truth, beauty and goodness. "It is imperative to evangelize cultures in order to inculturate the Gospel." (EG, n. 69)

- Social Sector: Encountering Christ in the stability of personal relationships and the protection of the family unit. "The family is the fundamental cell of society." (EG, n. 66)

- The Economy: Encountering Christ in the just sharing of the world's resources. "...the powerful feed upon the powerless. As a consequence, masses of people find themselves excluded and marginalized...." (EG, n. 53)

- Technology and Scientific Research: Encountering Christ in ethical research. Science and faith are compatible: "Dialogue between science and faith also brings the work of evangelization at the service of peace." (EG, n. 242)

- Civic Life: Encountering Christ in authentic freedom and dialogue. "Evangelization also involves the path of dialogue ... dialogue with states, dialogues with society – including dialogue with cultures and the sciences – and dialogue with other believers who are not part of the Catholic Church." (EG, n. 238)

- Media and Social Communications: Encountering Christ in life-giving media and communications. There is a need for new approaches to evangelization. "There are ecclesial structures which can hamper efforts at evangelization, yet even good structures are only helpful when there is a life constantly driving, sustaining and assessing them." (EG, n. 26)

- Religion: Encountering Christ in catechesis and faith development. "We know well that with Jesus life becomes richer and that with him it is easier to find meaning in everything. This is why we evangelize." (EG, n. 266)

Let's explore some key issues that need to be assessed.

Culture: Encountering Christ in Truth, Beauty and Goodness

Where there are idols, God is not known. This is the insight communicated by St. Paul when he visits the Areopagus, the "Hill of Ares" in Athens (Acts 17:16-34). The Areopagus represented an important legal institution in Athenian culture. St. Paul's famous Areopagus sermon addresses his discovery of an altar with the following dedication: "To an unknown god." Paul says, "What therefore you worship as unknown, this I proclaim to you. The God who made the world and everything in it, he who is Lord of heaven and earth, does not live in shrines made by human hands" (Acts 17:24). During this mission, St. Paul discovers the many altars dedicated to a variety of gods. This altar to an unknown god ensured that no unknown gods be offended. St. Paul seizes the opportunity to engage the Athenian culture and challenge those present to reconsider the identity of this unknown god. St. Paul encourages the Athenians to encounter God, the Lord of heaven and earth. This is the God who raised Jesus from the dead. A few who heard the message left their community to follow Paul, including one member of the Areopagus, Dionysius.

What are the idols in today's culture that keep people from knowing God? Money? Fame? The Internet? Sex? Food? TV? The list can go on and on. Recall the woman at the well in John's Gospel (4:1-42); she learns that Jesus is the only encounter that does not leave a person thirsty. St. Teresa of Avila warned against the lust for status, as it keeps us in a constant state of anxiety. It can also leave a crack for evil to set in and consume us with thoughts of advancement and greed. Dr. Scott Peck's book *The People of the Lie* shares the psychology behind certain evil acts, and how they can begin with a lie. For example, consider this possible scenario[53]: a young man who has been ambitious all his life has desired nothing but status and fame. He lies on his resumé and secures a high-profile position with an organization. His resumé is based on a lie. While he is in a new position, he begins to steal ideas from others who are more learned and have more credentials. Eventually, he is offered a promotion and praise as a result. One day, someone new is hired and this person knows his history. The new worker knows the man lacks the credentials and integrity needed for his current position. He also knows that this man tends to lie and cheat his way to the top. He tries to expose the hypocrisy, but the man comes back swinging, scapegoating and slandering the one who dared to expose him, creating more evil and more lies. This is one example of how status can become an idol and moves us farther and farther away from God. The man who lied to get ahead demonstrated very clearly that God was not known. This is why Jesus refers to Satan as the "father of lies" (John 8:44).

The objects of our desires can become idols. In another book, *On Earth as it is in Heaven*, I explore the physiological and spiritual dimensions of addiction. Addiction to gambling, gaming and pornography affects a person's physiology as well as his or her mood, thoughts and behaviour. Dr. Norman Doidge has studied neuroplasticity and the effects of pornography on the brain.[54] Men have confessed that at the time they married their wives, they found them physically attractive and could be aroused by them. In a moment of weakness, a man may start to watch pornography and notice how his body and mind reacts to the images. Dr. Doidge shares that eventually, with frequent visits to pornography sites, the man's brain responds to these images and is aroused by them only to discover that intimacy with their spouses is changing or deteriorating. This leads to a frustrating cycle of compulsion, tolerance levels changing (needing more and more to satisfy, like an addiction to substances), denial, or even depression and self-loathing.[55] Habits and desires that do not bear the fruits of the Holy Spirit are destructive and make God less known. Similarly, Dr. Gerald May has studied alcoholism and its control over certain people. If they seek help, Dr. May suggests, God's grace can strengthen them so that they are no longer dominated by an affliction. His book *Addiction and Grace* has helped many rediscover joy and wholeness.

So how can we encounter God in the culture? We can encounter God in truth, beauty and goodness. These are properties of God's very being. As you continue to read, you may discover that one of these properties, or more, is your dominant transcendental language.[56]

ENCOUNTERING GOD THROUGH THE QUEST FOR TRUTH

"I am the way and the truth and the life." ∾ JOHN 14:6

God reveals truths to us through scripture and Tradition. These revealed truths make up what we call the deposit of faith, the fullness of God's truths revealed in Jesus Christ. Jesus handed on these truths to his apostles, and the deposit was sealed with the death of the last apostle. These truths were then handed on to the successors of the apostles, the bishops of our Church. Some of these truths were handed on by Jesus' companions in written form, although Jesus did not leave us any of his own writings, while other truths were unwritten, only to be explained and developed at a later date.

While the deposit is complete, it has at times taken centuries for our understanding of a certain truth to become complete. It is our understanding that needs development and completion, because truth cannot change. The pillars of Tradition consist of scripture, liturgy, liturgical art, early Christian writers, creeds and magisterial teaching.[57] We pray our belief and believe what we pray. The magisterium has interpreted the truths we find in scripture and given us a complete or clear understanding. Some truths in scripture are very explicit or clearly communicated; other truths both written and unwritten require the magisterium to offer a complete or final interpretation to the faithful.

Sometimes it takes years of prayer and reflection to receive a complete understanding of a revealed truth. Some truths revealed in scripture include the Ten Commandments, the Beatitudes, other teachings of Jesus, and the Resurrection of Jesus. There are other truths handed on to us through the other pillars of Tradition, namely, the Immaculate Conception of Mary and the Assumption of Mary, to name two. Scripture and Tradition are considered revealed law and make up a "single sacred deposit of the Word of God" (*Dogmatic Constitution on Divine Revelation,* 1965, n. 10).

Our understanding of some of these truths developed over centuries. We can also learn certain truths through what we call the Natural Law. In St. Paul's letter to the Romans, Paul refers to the way the Gentiles, who did not know the Law of Moses, are led by reason to know the law of God. This law is "written on their hearts," and they can use their informed conscience to know these moral and spiritual truths (see Romans 2:14-15). This inner dialogue is guided by the Holy Spirit, who inspires thoughts that lead to inspiration and encouragement, especially when we do something good, or to remorse, when we have hurt ourselves or others. The ability to feel remorse is the sign of a developed conscience.

Peace, as a fruit of the Holy Spirit, is an indicator of fruitful living. Our God-given ability to reason can give us access to certain truths about God's laws governing nature and individuals. Faith, according to St. Thomas Aquinas, gives us access to higher truths. Faith informed by reason is the ideal combination. The culture can inform conscience and desensitize us, persuading us to believe or act in a certain way without feeling remorse. Indeed, it is as Paul taught, that we have "exchanged the truth about God for a lie" (Romans 1:25).

Some historical commentators have noted that today's culture is very similar to the Roman culture in the days of Jesus and Paul. It is our duty as Christians to pursue the truth, and we have resources in scripture and Tradition to assist us. The "path" of encountering God through truth, however, may be more appealing to some than to others. Not everyone is drawn to this type of study or discernment. This path may appeal to you if you are a truth seeker, philosopher or theologian at heart. Truth may be your dominant transcendental language. You may be someone who loves to learn and read and pursue courses of interest. You may pay close attention to words and you may read widely. My guess is that St. Paul started out as a truth seeker. While there is an upside to this path, there may be the danger of being limited due to one's focus on study and sophisticated ways of thinking.

St. Paul encountered Christ after a period of great arrogance and pride, pursuing and attacking Christians. The irony is that he believed he was doing God's will. In the end, words or books did not convert St. Paul; rather, it was the love of Christ. The desire to pursue truth should begin with conversion. Paul himself reminds us that love is the greatest gift; even our intellects, as great as they are, can leave us all puffed up and arrogant. The resurrection is a reminder that truth will always be vindicated. Truth cannot be killed, nor can it be changed. Throughout the ages, some people have tried to control the access to truth; if it cannot be controlled, they have tried to silence it; when it cannot be silenced, they have tried to kill it by killing the messenger. This is why so many prophets have been murdered. The truth exposes lies and deception. If truth encounters humility in a person, that person receives the teaching and turns her life around. If truth encounters pride in a person, that person feels he is being attacked and exposed and will scapegoat and slander the messenger instead of risking exposure and correction.

The quest for truth implies the acceptance of truth. Unfortunately, pride and greed will resist the truth in order to maintain a lie. On the other hand, arrogance can be an obstacle as well. God is greater than the greatest intellect. St. Paul teaches that love, not the intellect, is stronger than death (see 1 Corinthians 13). In order to flourish in this path, it is important to surrender our intellect to the Holy Spirit, so that it can be refined and used to keep us humble and open to discovering truths through beauty and goodness. God's love will tame the person whose intellect tempts him to boast or to be "all puffed up." Reason alone leaves us limited in our understanding of God. On its own, reason cannot grant us access to the higher mysteries of our faith. Faith, hope and love, on the other hand, keep us close to the way of Jesus Christ and his truth. Faith and reason are compatible; truth cannot contradict truth. Jesus is the model because he is the way, the truth and the life (John 14:6). An encounter with Christ leads the way to the Father. An encounter with Christ is an encounter with the truth. An encounter with Jesus is an encounter with the fullness of life.

Encountering Christ in truth:

- Develop a reading list for parishioners
- Develop a diocesan/parish library that is open to the public
- Encourage the pursuit of courses or study nights

ENCOUNTERING GOD IN BEAUTY

"But, as it is written, 'What no eye has seen, nor ear heard, nor the human heart conceived, what God has prepared for those who love him'..." ∞ 1 CORINTHIANS 2:9

The Oxford Dictionary defines the word "beauty" as a "combination of qualities giving pleasure to the sight or other senses or to the mind." St. Thomas Aquinas reminds us that knowledge can come through the senses.[58] The beauty of the liturgy, music, art, theatre and all of God's creation, including the natural world – all of these can stimulate and feed the senses, leading us to feel transported. Some people may discover that beauty is their dominant transcendental language. Culture can form the person or deform the person, depending on exposure to beauty, truth and goodness.

Youth are influenced by many images, propaganda and hidden agendas. It is interesting how the minds of our young people are being influenced by the type of music they listen to. Do you feel agitated or uplifted after you listen to music on your MP3 player or the radio? In 1967, Dr. Alfred A. Tomatis, a French doctor, was asked to treat a group of Benedictine monks who were experiencing fatigue and depression. He discovered that they had reduced the number of hours they would spend chanting. When he asked them to go back to the original number of hours spent chanting, their symptoms were alleviated.[59] Dr. Tomatis's research on the neurophysiological effect of Gregorian chant on the mind revealed the benefits of chanting and listening to beautiful music. Regular chanting and exposure to beautiful music led to increased feelings of overall well-being.

Now you may be thinking, "I am not trained to chant and I do not have the time to chant." While we are not expected to live in community the same way, like the Benedictines, we need life-giving sounds and community. The above example demonstrates the impact of beautiful music on the whole person. Even though we may not have the time to chant on a regular basis, we can limit the kinds of sounds to which we are exposed. Some sounds are just noise, while others feed us. We should keep this in mind when it comes to our children and the video games they play. The music in the background can lead to agitation.[60] My youngest son recently suffered a concussion. It was early spring. He was playing soccer and tripped over the ball, which led to his head hitting the frozen ground, not once but twice. The doctor in the emergency room at a local hospital told us to keep things quiet for at least three days: no music, no television, no video games, no bright lights. In order for his brain to heal, it could not be exposed to certain sounds or made to process anything. After a few days, we could gradually introduce a few activities. Silence clearly helps the brain heal after a concussion.[61]

Donald F. Roberts, Peter G. Christenson and Douglas A. Gentile have published a chapter entitled "The Effects of Violent Music on Children and Adolescents" in *Media Violence and Children: A Complete Guide for Parents and Professionals.*[62] The authors admit that music "has become more aggressive and edgy over the decades."[63] They have studied and consulted the studies of other researchers on the effects of violent music on children and adolescents. They found that "angry-sounding" music may produce aggressive thoughts and feelings, especially if the child is at risk.[64] While most heavy metal fans would not be considered at-risk youth, the authors found "those youth who are troubled or at risk tend overwhelmingly to embrace heavy metal."[65]

> "With regard to school, heavy metal fans report more conflict with teachers and other school authorities and perform less well academically than those whose tastes run more to the mainstream ... they tend to be distant from their families and are often at odds with their parents." ∞ ROBERTS, CHRISTENSON, AND GENTILE, *MEDIA VIOLENCE AND CHILDREN*, P. 160

In conclusion, they found that the "emotional sound" of the music, whether it is heavy metal or Christian heavy metal, has an effect on the listeners.[66] Other violent and visual media tend to have a powerful effect on viewers as well, eliciting fear and anxiety. Where has the beauty gone? In contrast, the "emotional sound" of Gregorian chant or classical music would be healing. With some school boards cutting arts programs, it is clear that other media outlets are satisfying the need for arts and entertainment. As Christians, it is time to take back beauty and challenge school boards to sustain programs that are life-giving, exposing students to beautiful sights and sounds that heal, not destroy.

It is well known that Pope John Paul II was an actor before he began to study for the priesthood. The dramatic arts can be used to feed people and inspire a faith journey. Movies such as *Bella* and *The Secret Garden* are examples of productions that inspire thinking about moral issues and the possibility for redemption. The Church needs faith-filled people to offer their gifts to the arts so that God's beauty can be experienced. Those working in these industries need to undergo a good examination of conscience to consider whether they are using their gifts to building a culture of life or a "culture of death."[67]

Even though not all are called to priesthood or religious life, we are all called to holiness. You can live out your call to holiness by using your gift in the arts, pleasing the senses and offering a foretaste of the heavenly kingdom. One of my favorite pieces of music is the *Agnus Dei* set to Samuel Barber's *Adagio for Strings*. It calms me and calms others when I use it in retreats or conferences. The path to God through beauty may appeal to those who are not drawn to books or reading. They need to see and sense in other ways. Their minds may be renewed as they use their senses to gather information regarding the laws of nature and creation. They may sense the beauty of God after chanting, visiting a beautiful cathedral or attending mass. Proposition 35 for the Synod on the New Evangelization notes that the liturgy "is the primary and most powerful expression of the New Evangelization ... The liturgy is not just a human action but an encounter with God which leads to contemplation and deepening friendship with God. In this sense, the liturgy of the Church is the best school of faith." We need to examine those parts of our culture that are not feeding the masses. In some ways, people are deprived due to the types of music, theatre and film that assault the senses instead of satisfying them. The beauty of God can be experienced in persons as well. It is a delight to sense God's presence in others, as they care for others, when they pray, when they show loving-kindness. Jesus' goodness and love made him beautiful. He reminds us of our true form, not necessarily physically perfect by the world's standards, but whole in Christ.

"It is my duty to profess my love for Jesus Christ and to profess the love Jesus Christ has for me." ⌒ SINGER/ARTIST J. MARK MCVEY, WHO PLAYED JEAN VALJEAN IN *LES MISÉRABLES* ON BROADWAY

"This fundamental role of beauty urgently needs to be restored in Christianity. In this regard, the new evangelization has an important role to play. The Church recognizes that human beings cannot exist without beauty. For Christians, beauty is found in the Paschal Mystery, in the transparency of the reality of Christ." ∾ *INSTRUMENTUM LABORIS*, N. 157

Love forms the person and makes her attractive. This wholeness manifests itself when a person is open to the work of the Holy Spirit in her life. Slowly but surely, the person experiences a restructuring of her personality and an inner transformation. Jesus is gradually reproduced in the person. Popular Christian speaker Joyce Meyer once described her early years before her conversion. In one of her television broadcasts, she shared that she was such a negative and cranky person, she would get a "cramp" just thinking a positive thought. She went on to describe the work of the Holy Spirit in her life over a 30-year period. She remains a unique personality, but she has been refined and healed. She is getting closer to her true self, her true form. Just as Jesus is the New Adam, she is becoming the New Joyce.

Michael Brown, editor of *Spirit Daily*, shared the following story of the conversion of a firefighter who had fallen into some bad habits that were disfiguring him. In a rare mystical moment, he encounters a vision of his restored self, his true form desired by God and revealed by Christ:

> We also recall a New York fireman we knew who had a drinking problem and was overdoing it at an annual firemen's picnic upstate. Intoxicated, he'd wandered up a training platform and before he knew it was stumbling off – ready to plummet several stories below (and perhaps to his end).
>
> At the last moment, as he tumbled off, he said, a hand grabbed him and yanked him back up onto the platform with one amazing motion. To his astonishment, he was looking at a stranger who was a mirror image of himself – but dressed far more neatly and very clean-shaven, far different than the disheveled fireman. It was as if this mysterious angel was showing him how he could and should be. The man simply disappeared immediately after (and the fireman cleaned up his act; we always ran into him at daily Mass).[68]

Whether you believe this story or not, wouldn't it be wonderful if our true, restored selves could be revealed to us in a sneak preview? How encouraging would that be? The good news is we have Jesus Christ who shows us what the restored person acts like, how he thinks, and how he loves. He encourages us to put on a "new nature." Jesus is beauty's true form. He reveals beauty and goodness to us. The need to experience and see goodness is a universal one.

Encountering Christ in beauty:

- Organize church tours/expose people to beautiful church architecture
- Use sacred music for prayer and meditation
- Buy sacred music for friends as gifts
- Support the work of iconographers and other liturgical artists
- Meditate on the beauty of God's creation
- Strive to reveal the beauty of Jesus in your character

ENCOUNTERING GOD THROUGH THE GOODNESS OF OTHERS

"Blessed are the pure of heart, for they shall see God." ∽ MATTHEW 5:8

I have a wonderful friend, Leanne, who would certainly fit the profile of a person who has found God through the quest for truth and through an appreciation for beauty. What sets her apart, however, is her goodness. Leanne prays for me every day and is the first to think about the needs of others. Those who know her speak very highly of her and affirm her beautiful faith and qualities. People sense God's goodness when they are in her presence.

Some people can be moved by the loving-kindness of others. The Parable of Nations in the Gospel of Matthew reminds us that love of neighbour leads to eternal life: "Truly I tell you, just as you did it to one of the least of these who are members of my family, you did it to me" (Matthew 25:40). We could easily provide new scenarios and examine our thoughts and actions, assessing whether we did see Christ in others and remembered doing things for him – or not:

- I was alone in a nursing home without visitors for three weeks and you came to visit me.

- I could not pay my mortgage payment and risked losing my house and you loaned me money.

- I was the victim of gossip and rumours and you defended me.

- I worked with you and shared my gifts, but you sabotaged me at every angle.

- I confided in you and you betrayed me.

The list can go on and on. Jesus came into the world not only because he is our model of holiness, not only because we are called to be partakers in his divine nature, not only to save and reconcile us with God, but because God loves us and desires us to know the love of God:[69] to show us how to love our neighbour.

The Parable of the Judgment of Nations and the conversion of St. Paul have a lot in common. In the Parable, Jesus reminds us that when we give drink to the thirsty and engage in other corporal acts of mercy, we do so for him. This serves as a reminder of the dignity of each person, one of our Catholic social teaching principles. It is also a reminder that we are created in the image and likeness of God, which is another Catholic social teaching principle. As Saul, the Hebrew version of Paul's name, was approaching Damascus, a flash of heavenly light surprised him and he fell to the ground, hearing these words, "Saul, Saul, why do you persecute me?" When Paul asked for the source of the voice to identify himself, the reply is "I am Jesus, whom you are persecuting" (Acts 9:4-5). These words would go on to inspire Paul's ecclesiology or theology of the church.

Paul is introduced to us as a man of violence; he is arrogant and abusive. He viciously attacked Christians and condemned them for believing that Jesus was the Messiah, the Christ. Before his conversion, he is described as "breathing threats and murder against the disciples of the Lord" (Acts 9:1). He was on his way to Damascus "so that if he found any who belonged to the Way, men or women, he might bring them bound to Jerusalem" (Acts 9:2). Hearing the words "Saul, Saul, why do you persecute me?" must have surprised him, especially once the identity of the voice was revealed to him.

First, as a Pharisee, he would have believed that the deceased slept in a state or underworld known as *Sheol*, where they would await the coming of the Messiah to free them from their sleep and bring them into the heavenly kingdom. Hearing Jesus reveal his identity as the Messiah challenged Paul to review his history of violence and abuse. This moment challenges him to reconsider Jesus as the Messiah. He may have thought to himself, "I did not persecute Jesus. I never met the guy! I persecuted Stephen and others, not Jesus." He comes to learn the great insight of the Parable of the Judgment of Nations; Jesus reminds us of the dignity of each person, and how we are called to love one another. Jesus is asking Paul to substitute the name of the Messiah for the names of the persecuted. You are persecuting the Son of God, the anointed one. What a revelation! This insight went on to inform the ecclesiology we find in Paul's letters, especially 1 Corinthians: "For just as the body is one and has many members, and all members of the body, though many, are one body, so it is with Christ" (1 Corinthians 12:12).

The body of Christ cannot be divided; this is why we are one. Paul learned that he was persecuting the body of Christ with his arrogance and violent temper. He believed he was doing God's will and thought this justified the violence: he believed it had to be done. It was the encounter with Christ's love and goodness that changed him. Christ showed him mercy and appointed him an apostle, meaning "one who is sent." He refers to himself as an apostle and goes on three challenging missions to preach the good news to the Gentiles, the non-Jews. The goodness and mercy of Jesus Christ inspired one of the most famous conversion stories of all time. Love teaches in ways that hate cannot. Love teaches in ways that the intellect cannot. While the intellect gives us access to certain truths, only love can transform. Love shows us how to be good citizens of the Kingdom. St. Paul teaches us what love is and what love is not. Love is the source of all goodness.

Consider the following examination of conscience based on 1 Corinthians 13:4-13. St. Paul starts his reflection on love by reminding us that love is superior to all other spiritual gifts. Whether they involve speaking in tongues, prophecy or deep faith, they are nothing without love. Even though you may attract and woo others with these gifts, they will not sustain relationships without love. Without love we have nothing.

Love is patient: Are you patient with your loved ones, knowing they may have vulnerabilities you do not have, and vice versa? Howard Storm is a Christian pastor who experienced a conversion due to a near-death experience. His story is available and accessible on YouTube and in his book, *My Descent into Death*. He, like St. Paul, was obnoxious and arrogant before his conversion. He was a professor at that time, and he shares that he was quite abrupt and rude to a nun who was a student in his art history class. He made it clear to her that he did not want her to share anything about faith and religion in class: "There'll be none of that here!" Many years after his conversion, he ran into her; after telling her about his conversion, he apologized for his behaviour. She said something like "It's about time. I have not stopped praying for you!" She was patient with her prayers and God gave her the grace to see the fruits of her efforts. In his near-death experience, Howard Storm was shown those occasions in which he was patient and the very many occasions in which he was not. He was allowed to see the ripple effect of his actions and this led to great remorse.

Love is kind: Are you meek and mild in your daily interactions? Do you think before you speak? Does your tone or choice of words upset your spouse, your colleagues, your neighbours? Do your words build them up? We are kind when others feel God's love through our words and actions.

Here are eight things love is *not*:

Envious: Do you take the time to assess your own giftedness? Do you suffer due to self-loathing? Do you envy the gifts and accomplishments of others? Envy is dangerous and can damage relationships. Envy can lead to disaster, even death: the envy of Cain led to the murder of Abel (Genesis 4:3-8); his brothers' envy led to the enslavement of Joseph (Genesis 37:11, 28); the envy and jealousy of the crowd was one of the factors contributing to the crucifixion of Jesus: "For he realized that it was out of jealousy that they handed him over" (Matthew 27:18). At the very least, your envy may be a stumbling block for another person who wants to use his or her gifts; at worst, it may be destructive and dangerous. St. Thomas Aquinas said that the worst form of jealousy is to be jealous of the spiritual gifts of another.

Boastful: Do you boast about your own strengths, gifts and accomplishments while putting others down? Do you blame family members or co-workers for any perceived limitations? Are you humble enough to acknowledge the gifts you have? Do you need to be praised for your actions or accomplishments? One translation of 1 Corinthians 13 reads: "love does not parade itself." Do you give out of love or for the recognition? Can you be anonymous in your giving?

Arrogant: Are you approachable and humble? Or do you place yourself and your own interests above all others? Do you see God's hand in your giftedness and accomplishments? Another translation reads: "love is not puffed up." Are you focused on yourself? Love stretches us and puts the focus on the other; it is not self-serving. To be arrogant is to have a "big head." Some are guilty of a "pride of grace," a sort of "look at me" approach to spirituality, like the Pharisee in the parable of the tax collector and the Pharisee (Luke 18:9-14). We may spend our time pointing out everyone else's faults without taking the time to work on ourselves.

Rude: Are you thoughtful and caring? Or are you abrupt and rude in your daily interactions? St. Paul teaches: "Be angry but do not sin; do not let the sun go down on your anger, and do not make room for the devil" (Ephesians 4:26-27). Love is kind, not rude.

Insisting on its own way: Do you want to get your way when there is a conflict? Or have you sacrificed any of your own desires to be there for your spouse and family?

Irritable: Does your mood influence the mood of the home? Are you able to bring stress to prayer so as not to punish those around you with your own irritation? Are you easily provoked?

Resentful: Do you resent the call to sacrifice in marriage, parenting, the single state or the ordained state? Do you resent pouring yourself out for your family? Or do you relate to Christ and his own pouring out with great love for us? Do you hold onto past hurts without trying to understand your loved ones? Have you asked for the grace to be open to the process of forgiveness? Has your heart hardened over the years? Do you hold grudges? Have you prayed to be understood and to understand?

Rejoicing in wrongdoing: Do you seize every opportunity to point out the shortcomings of others? Do you tear others down in order to feel better about yourself? Have you secretly rejoiced in the downfall of others? Have you prayed for those who hurt you or others? Have you prayed to know the truth?

Love ...

Rejoices in truth: When in the midst of a conflict, do you pray to confront truthfully yet tactfully? Truth sets us free, and we owe it to our loved ones and friends to point out any habits or words that are not life-giving. Truth builds the relationship and leads to transformation. Truth is the language of the Holy Spirit and love is its power. Can you receive correction?

Bears all things: Except for lies and abuse – these need to be addressed with great care and wisdom. Pick your battles and ask for the patience to deal with the little annoyances in life.

Believes all things: Do you believe God loves you and desires your happiness and transformation? Do you believe you can be healed and transformed? Do you believe that past hurts can be redeemed? It is a lie to believe you cannot be forgiven.

Hopes all things: Has some past hurt robbed you of your joy and hope? Pray to be released from the bondage of the past and fear of the future. St. Paul reminds us that hope is like a helmet for the mind, the helmet of salvation. Hope protects the mind from fear and anxiety. Wise optimism leads to confidence in the future.

Endures all things: Love conquers all. Perfect love casts out all fear (1 John 4:18), but perfect fear casts out love. The power of God's love, the Holy Spirit, raised Jesus from the dead. The same power can conquer adversity and pain in our own lives. Thanks to God's grace, we will not be dominated by our afflictions. When we do not surrender our afflictions to God, they tend to dominate our thinking and very being.

Love never ends.

Faith, hope and charity: These are the theological virtues. St. Paul tells us that faith and charity are a breastplate for the heart, and hope is a helmet for the mind. Let us remember to ask for help, to pray and to see others the way God sees them: worthy of love and redemption.

A pastor once said that it is easy to substitute the name of Jesus for love: Jesus is patient and kind. Jesus does not envy. Can you substitute your name in the text? Does it describe you? Paul includes this chapter in his discussion of spiritual gifts to remind the Corinthians that love is the greatest gift. It is love that reveals the true identity of a person, not other gifts. Love remains the greatest gift because it takes the focus off ourselves. It is the true measure of spiritual greatness. The Corinthians were enamoured with spiritual gifts. St. Paul reminds them that the "awe" factor should not detract them from the love of God. All other gifts can come to an end, but "love never ends." Love is an attribute of God (1 John 4:8) that can be known. The Parable of the Judgment of Nations in Matthew (25:31-46) reminds us that only love is rewarded in the afterlife.

Try writing a short version of 1 Corinthians 13 based on your own life and experience. Here is the potential version of a very learned person:

> Though I have a Ph.D. or a graduate degree in Theology and know the *Catechism of the Catholic Church* inside out, but have not love, I know nothing. Though I speak many languages and am quite articulate, but have not love, I say nothing. Though I believe in God and attend weekly mass, but have not love, I believe nothing. Love forms us and uses our gifts for the common good. My intellect may fail me; my speaking ability may diminish or be impeded by illness; I may lose my job; love, on the other hand never ends.

"God is love." ∾ 1 JOHN 4:8

We encounter God when we encounter love, because love of neighbour reveals God in families and communities. The Song of Solomon (8:6) affirms that "love is as strong as death," but the resurrection reminds us that love conquers death. Love of our neighbour spills over into the social sector.

Encountering Christ in goodness:

- If your state of life allows, volunteer your time and gifts to a local agency
- Assess your gifts and serve through your natural giftedness
- Affirm the gifts of others
- Pray that others sense the goodness of our Lord through your charitable acts
- Glorify God, not yourself. Mary magnified the Lord (Luke 1:46)

Social Sector: Encountering Christ in Families and Migrants

"The boundaries between pastoral care of the faithful, new evangelization and specific missionary activity are not clearly definable, and it is unthinkable to create barriers between them or to put them into watertight compartments." ∾ POPE JOHN PAUL II, *REDEMPTORIS MISSIO*, N. 34

In the above quote, Pope John Paul II explains how missionary activity, catechetical activity and pastoral activity are all part of the Church's evangelizing mission. Different people in different situations will need to be fed in different ways, according to their state of life and changing needs. The social sector addresses the needs of families, migrants and other vulnerable people. All of these people need an encounter with Christ.

FAMILIES

We encounter Christ in this sector in the form of Catholic social teaching, marriage preparation, other family ministries, and pastoral care. The working document on the New Evangelization acknowledges that families need support and need to feel part of a community (*Instrumentum Laboris*, n. 111). Pope Francis has called for an upcoming Synod of Bishops, which will have a two-staged itinerary: "firstly, an Extraordinary General Assembly in 2014, ... and secondly, an Ordinary General Assembly in 2015 to seek working guidelines in the pastoral care of the person and the family" (Synod of Bishops, *Pastoral Challenges to the Family in the Context of Evangelization* [Preparatory Document], 2013).

I often remark on how the formation process for the two sacraments of service, marriage and ordination to the priesthood, varies so drastically. Men in formation for the permanent diaconate or the priesthood will spend from four to eight years or more being formed in the following areas: intellectual, pastoral, human and spiritual. They have spiritual directors who journey with them and whole communities that pray for them. They are given at least one year to experience full-time parish life to be sure that this state of life is the right one for them. They are given several opportunities to understand the life of a priest or deacon. While these opportunities do not exhaust the day-to-day reality of priesthood, they do give some insight into the experience.

When it comes to preparation for the sacrament of marriage, depending on your diocese and those who assist with the ministry to the engaged, preparation may consist of a weekend or a two-hour evening session for six to eight weeks. For several years I worked as a chaplaincy leader in an alternative high school working with at-risk youth. The students were given an opportunity to take a course on healthy dating. I thought to myself, why do we have to wait for our youth to be at risk before we talk to them about healthy dating? Having sex at a young age and before marriage can lead a person to bond prematurely to the wrong person for an indefinite period of time. Dr. Daniel Amen tells us that bonding hormones are released when couples are intimate, and the brain changes. He goes on to say that infatuation can last anywhere from months to several years. Our physiology and neurobiology are affected by our behaviour, locking us into inappropriate relationships.[70]

> "Sex outside marriage tries to 'say' two contradictory things at the same time: on the one hand, I give my entire physical self to you; on the other hand, I have not made a total (exclusive and irrevocable) gift of myself to you." ⌒ PATRICIA MURPHY, *CATHOLIC MARRIAGE: AN INTIMATE COMMUNITY OF LIFE AND LOVE* [TORONTO: NOVALIS, 2011], 46.

Let's look at what the statistics reveal regarding marriage and divorce. In 2012 the U.S. government's *National Survey of Family Growth* estimated a 40–50% chance that a marriage will end in divorce. Some reasons for these divorces include:

- "running out of steam" or falling out of love
- communication breakdown
- unreasonable behaviour
- infidelity
- midlife crisis
- financial issues
- physical, psychological or emotional abuse

Similarly, Dr. John Gottman is known for his research on communication and divorce prediction. He has found that criticism, defensiveness, contempt and stonewalling can lead to divorce.

Marriage preparation should really begin in the early years of a child's formation. Regardless of whether the child gets married in the future, there are skills that can be learned and gained that will help with all future relationships. Research conducted by the Women's Legal Action Education fund has found that 52% of single-parent families are headed by women who live in poverty. Even with a declaration of nullity, divorced individuals may need help with healing, studying old patterns and wounds. Various diocesan offices offer excellent programs for divorced and widowed Catholics in need of healing and hope, preparing them for the possibility of future relationships. Elizabeth Einstein has done some tremendous work with ministering to step/blended families. Second marriages require preparation and support, and all marriages require lifelong support and prayer.

Dr. Mark Butler has discovered the spiritual, psychological and physical benefits of prayer in marriage. Prayer and a deepened faith can assist couples with day-to-day challenges. It gives us resilience and spiritual stamina. We have direction in scripture: Mary, in the story of the wedding at Cana, says, "Do whatever he tells you." What does Jesus tell us about relationships and communication?

- Hardness of heart (grudges/resentment) can kill any relationship (Matthew 19:8)
- Go quickly to reconcile; don't wait due to fear or pride (Matthew 5:23-24)
- Love one another (John 13:34)
- Be meek and mild like him (Matthew 11:28-30)
- Forgive one another (sin is like debt; we owe something when we have hurt someone: an apology restores that which has been taken, humility) (Matthew 6:12)
- Look at your own faults and vulnerabilities before you attack someone else (Matthew 7:3-5)
- Do not judge (we can judge situations/actions, not persons; we each have our own vulnerabilities) (Matthew 7:1-2)
- Develop self-discipline around attraction to others; thoughts may lead to actions (Matthew 5:28)
- Include Jesus in the relationship (John 2:5)

We can add the wisdom of Paul to the list:

- Be equally yoked or well matched (premature or premarital sex can complicate this one) (2 Corinthians 6:14)
- A believing wife's prayers and actions can lead to her husband's conversion, and vice versa (1 Corinthians 7:14)
- Marriage is a mystery that reflects Christ's love for the Church (Ephesians 5:21-33)
- Husbands and wives are to submit to one another (Ephesians 5:21-33)
- Confront truthfully yet tactfully, not abusively, whenever the situation demands it (Ephesians 4:26)
- Be patient and kind (1 Corinthians 13:4)

Self-knowledge and knowledge of one's spouse can help here as well. Dr. Gary Chapman's best-selling book *The Five Love Languages* argues that there may be communication and conflict management problems in a marriage due to lack of knowing oneself and one's spouse. He suggests that most individuals have a dominant love language and may use this to judge their partners. They may be tempted to project their own language onto their partners, only to be disappointed when their partner is not as fluent in this language. He discovered that most people have one or more of these five love languages:

1. Words

2. Quality time

3. Touch

4. Gifts

5. Acts of service[71]

Consider the situation where someone with words as a love language is paired with someone whose love language consists of gifts. The "gifts" person spends months planning for the perfect gift for their upcoming anniversary. The "words" person opens it and says, "You spent too much money. Return it!" The words person may have preferred a card with a poem or other nice sentiments. Chapman says that not everyone has an easy time with words, so they will find other ways to demonstrate their love for their loved ones. How many of us have had arguments with our loved ones due to misunderstanding and projection? Chapman says we should make the effort to understand our spouse's love language and speak it from time to time.

There is a story about a married couple. (I may have some of the details wrong, but I think I have the general sense of it.) This couple, married for decades, has enjoyed having sandwiches for lunch on a regular basis. The husband would make his wife's lunch using the ends of the loaf. Finally, one day, after many years, the wife erupted, saying, "Why do you make my sandwich with the end pieces? I hate the end pieces!" The husband, with great sorrow, replied, "I love the end pieces. They are my favourite. I gave them up for you. I thought that they would be your favorite, too, since I like them so much." What the wife perceived as thoughtlessness was really her husband sacrificing what he loved, thinking she loved it, too.

To go so many years without communicating our needs is not uncommon in some relationships. Fear and pride may keep us from telling our loved ones what we need; yet they are not mind readers. How many of us have said, "Well, it comes easily to me; why can't you do it?" These are skills and insights that need to be developed well before the wedding day. Mandatory courses in the area of conflict management and communication can save couples years of turmoil. There are skilled professionals available who can help with this process. It is an insult to this sacrament of service to limit preparation to a weekend or eight sessions. We owe it to couples to offer support and resources well before their wedding date. It would be ideal to include courses or units of study at the high school level.

The family is the "domestic church" and is in need of healing and support. It needs to be protected. My pastor once said, "All states of life are called to support and protect the family." Priesthood serves families. Whether they are new immigrants or well-established families in a community, we need qualified individuals who can offer a variety of social ministries and pastoral care. We can diminish the need for these services with early prevention, including mandatory communication and conflict management courses and healthy dating seminars at the high school level; studying the leading factors contributing to divorce; sharing the research on the benefits of saving sex for marriage; encouraging training in the area of effective parenting styles; studying the needs of migrants; and expanding the marriage preparation course. The Church needs to tap into existing social services and use the research and programs that are bearing fruit. Parents need to lobby their school boards and the U.S. Department of Education and ask for these services or programs.

It would be ideal to offer a required course at the high school level followed by a year-long course offered by the local church in preparation for marriage. The marriage preparation course should include expanded units in the areas of communication and conflict management, forgiveness and reconciliation, sexual intimacy, finances, and self-knowledge. The sign performed by Jesus at the wedding at Cana in John's Gospel affirms that marriages can be transformed when Jesus is included in the relationship (John 2:1-11). Mary says, "Do whatever he tells you." His teaching and love can mould us into the best version of ourselves.

MIGRANTS

Another group targeted in this sector, in need of an encounter with Christ, includes migrants.

> "... the treatment of the **phenomenon of the great migration** which is causing an increasing number of people to leave their country of origin to live in urban settings, resulting in a meeting and mixing of cultures and contributing to the erosion of basic reference points in life. Joined to the spread of secularization, this process causes a situation of extreme cultural liquidity, which increasingly leaves less room for long standing traditions, including religious ones." ∾ *INSTRUMENTUM LABORIS*, N. 55.

Immigration policy is a controversial topic. With war, natural disaster and regime collapse occurring in more and more nations, refugees are in need of safe passage and countries that will accommodate their needs and concerns for safety. Some countries have been struggling to find the just and ethical approach to the problem of undocumented workers. Recent changes in immigration policies in the United States have led the US Conference of Catholic Bishops and others to voice their concerns over the ethical dilemmas created by such policies. Father Sean Carroll, a Jesuit priest, is the executive director of the Kino Border Initiative. This initiative serves those who are deported on both sides of the U.S.–Mexico border in Nogales, Arizona, and Nogales, Sonora. It provides shelter and food as well as serving as advocates for immigration reform.

Father Carroll testified before the US Congress, sharing the horrors of American immigration policies. He noted that the Department of Homeland Security's Alien Transfer Exit Program has had devastating effects on family unity: "We at the Kino Border Initiative watch in disbelief as we receive women deported to Nogales, Mexico, while their husbands are repatriated to distant points of entry along the U.S.-

Mexican border."[72] He goes on to talk about the trauma these women experience away from their husbands, putting them at risk of exploitation and violence. The children of these undocumented citizens, many of whom are American citizens, are removed from their parents and left with other family members or placed in foster care.

> "In the first six months of 2011, the U.S. government removed more than 46,000 mothers and fathers of U.S. citizens ... This reality falls short of what Scripture teaches regarding care for the widow, the orphan and the stranger. Our current policies essentially leave many children as orphans, wives and husbands as widows and widowers, and the stranger deported across the border, away from their family members who need them so deeply." ∾ FATHER SEAN CARROLL, SJ

Can you imagine the trauma of these children apprehended by the authorities and separated from their parents? Perhaps even separated from their siblings? Can you imagine the trauma of these spouses separated at the border? Why the need to separate spouses? Where does one encounter Christ in this sector, in this situation? The U.S. bishops have called the authorities to a higher level of ethical standards when it comes to the treatment of undocumented workers.

> "It is a fundamental inversion of values when laws and politics place national interests before human dignity." ∾ MOST REVEREND ROGER EBACHER, ARCHBISHOP EMERITUS OF GATINEAU, CANADA

In 2001, the United States Conference of Catholic Bishops issued a pastoral statement, *Welcoming the Stranger Among Us: Unity in Diversity*. In 2013, they issued a statement, *The Catholic Church's Position on Immigration Reform*. Similarly, in 2006, the Canadian Conference of Catholic Bishops' Episcopal Commission for Social Affairs issued a pastoral letter on the plight of immigrants and refugees. The letter outlines a number of recommendations, including

- Introducing the appeal system for refugee claimants as required by Canadian Immigration Law

• Eliminating obstacles that impede the speedy reunification of families

• Being more welcoming of newcomers

• Improving protection for migrant workers.

With the Internet and other means of social communications, people around the world are becoming increasingly aware of the social and foreign policies of various nations. Globalization is connected to this sector. The authors of the working document for the synod note both the positive and the negative aspects of this social phenomenon. When it is linked to economy and production, it tends to generate a negative response. On the other hand, "it can also be viewed as a time of growth, in which humanity can learn to develop new forms of solidarity and new ways of sharing development for the good of all" (*Instrumentum Laboris*, n. 55). Surely there is a way to generate fair and just immigration policies that protect individual nations as well as the rights of those who are suffering and in need of safe passage and shelter. Canadian Archbishop emeritus Roger Ebacher, then chairman of the Episcopal Commission for Social Affairs, in an interview on the 2006 Pastoral Letter, stated: "refugees have become scapegoats in national security questions especially since September 11, 2001."[73] The many vulnerable victims of war are suffering due to the sins of others. As God's people, we have a duty to advocate for the oppressed and ensure that just policies govern the treatment of migrants.

While another author may have taken a different approach with this particular sector, I wanted to address marriage and the needs of all families – citizens and non-citizens. If families who are dealing with conflict are supported in their struggles, they will have the skills needed to deal with the next sector: the economy.

The Economy: Encountering Christ Through the Just Sharing of Resources

The inequality within and among nations has been addressed in many of the Church's social documents. The following are Catholic Social Teaching principles:

i. The human person is the Image of God

ii. Dignity of the human person

iii. The person is a social being

iv. The person is called to the Kingdom of God

v. Linking of the religious and social dimension of life

vi. Political and economic rights

vii. Option for the poor

viii. Link of love and justice

ix. Promotion of the common good as the mission of the Church

The increase in the gap between the rich and the poor, the inequality associated with the distribution of the world's resources, and the exploitation of God's creation are areas targeted in this sector. (See *Instrumentum Laboris*, n. 56.) How do we encounter Christ in this sector?

- Sharing of the world's resources

- Just leadership

- Ethical laws governing international financial monetary systems

The 2009 United Nations Development Report noted that half of the world's population, nearly three billion people, lives on less than $2 per day. The same report declared that nearly a billion people entered the 21st century unable to read a book or sign their names. Twenty percent of the population, living in the developed nations, consumes 86 percent of the world's goods. Approximately 790 million people in the developing world, almost two thirds of whom reside in Asia and the Pacific region, are still chronically undernourished. According to recent UNICEF findings, 30,000 children die each day due to poverty.

In 2011, the Pontifical Council for Justice and Peace published "Reforming the International Financial and Monetary Systems," which addressed the current global banking crisis. The Council concludes that the crisis is due to selfishness, collective greed and the "hoarding of goods on a great scale."[74]

In one example, access to water is being controlled and manipulated. The state of Michigan has new water withdrawal laws, allowing water to be withdrawn to be used as bottled water. According to the Beverage Marketing Corporation, sales of bottled water reached $10.9 billion dollars in 2006. Michael C. Bellas, chairman and CEO of this corporation, says that by 2020, bottled water will surpass soft drinks as the top-selling beverage.[75] With clean drinking water running low in several regions, bottled water is in high demand. This means that water has been exploited and made more easily accessible to the wealthy, limiting access for the poor. Sources of clean drinking water continue to be sold and privatized, restricting access for local residents.

Farmers' access to seeds has been affected as well. Increasingly, seeds are genetically modified, and large corporations are taking more control.[76] In an article on genetically engineered seeds, Colin Todhunter explains that over 90 to 95% of all cotton grown in India is now genetically modified "and controlled by big corporations."[77] He goes on to report that in India alone, 250,000 farmers have committed suicide since 1997. Researchers "report that farmers experience one of the highest rates of suicide in any industry, and there is growing evidence that those involved in farming are at higher risk of developing mental health problems."[78] As they lose more and more control and autonomy, they feel enslaved and manipulated by the greed of large corporations. There is also the controversy over genetically engineered "terminator seeds." According to Todhunter, these seeds are engineered "to make them sterile and unusable for replanting, resulting in farmers having to buy new seeds."[79] While there are worldwide discussions around the legalities associated with this practice, there are ethical concerns that need to be addressed as well. If this practice is endorsed, farmers will be reduced to buying these genetically engineered seeds and the consumer will be eating the produce generated by these seeds.

Farmers are losing more and more control of their industry, and God's creation continues to be exploited and manipulated. The laws of nature are being rewritten before our very eyes. Pope Francis believes that "the idolatry of money" has created this sinful situation:

> One cause of this situation is found in our relationship with money, since we calmly accept its dominion over ourselves and our societies. The current financial crisis can make us overlook the fact that it originated in a profound human crisis: the denial of the primacy of the human person! We have created new idols. The worship of the ancient golden calf (cf. Ex. 32:1-35) has returned in a new and ruthless guise in the idolatry of money and the dictatorship of an impersonal economy lacking a truly human purpose. The worldwide crisis affecting finance and the economy lays bare their imbalances and, above all, their lack of real concern for human beings; man is reduced to one of his needs alone: consumption. (*Evangelii Gaudium*, n. 55)

In Matthew's account of the Lord's Prayer (6:9-13), the petition for daily bread is strategically placed after the call to do God's will. If everyone did God's will when it comes to the sharing and fair distribution of the world's resources, many more would have their daily bread. Seeds and water would not be hoarded and controlled for mass profit, benefiting the few. Banking systems would be monitored, and those who manipulate and steal would be disciplined. This is how we encounter Christ in this sector: through love of neighbour, just sharing of resources, and the exposure of lies and hypocrisy.

Economy, as the very word indicates, should be the art of achieving a fitting management of our common home, which is the world as a whole. Each meaningful economic decision made in one part of the world has repercussions everywhere else; consequently, no government can act without regard for shared responsibility. Indeed, it is becoming increasingly difficult to find local solutions for enormous global problems which overwhelm local politics with difficulties to resolve. If we really want to achieve a healthy world economy, what is needed at this juncture in history is a more efficient way of interacting which, with due regard for the sovereignty of each nation, ensures the economic well-being of all countries, not just a few. ᗑ *EVANGELII GAUDIUM*, N. 206

Technology and Scientific Research:
Encountering Christ in Ethical Research

> "The only limit to scientific progress is in preserving the dignity of the human person created in God's image, who must always be actively involved in scientific research and technology and never be a mere object of study." ∾ *INSTRUMENTUM LABORIS*, N. 156

Whenever I look up the Pontifical Academy for the Sciences on the Internet, I am surprised to see the number of projects supported by the Church. Some people may be surprised to see how much the Church affirms the relationship between science and faith. Some basic principles support this relationship:

- Faith can never conflict with reason.

- Truth cannot contradict truth.

- Faith and reason are compatible.

- There are truths we attain through our use of reason, and there are truths we attain through our experience with faith.

- There is an organic link between theology, philosophy, and natural sciences.

This relationship can be distorted through extremes, however. One extreme is scientism, which holds that no valid knowledge can be received outside of the sciences. This position sees no place for faith; the rational mind does not benefit from it. There is an exaggerated emphasis on scientific findings. The other extreme consists of people of faith who mistrust the scientific community. Faith and science together can produce great fruit and deepen our understanding of the laws of nature:

- Science can benefit from theology.

- Faith can be of benefit to science.

- Theology can benefit from science (natural science can eliminate factual error from theology).

- Together, the book of faith (the scriptures) and the book of nature (natural law) reveal God.

Pope John Paul II taught that reason gains its true meaning only when it is understood from the context of faith (*Fides et Ratio*, 1998). Catholic theologians, Catholic educators, clergy and all who teach Catholic education need to be aware of the scientific developments of our day. Dr. Margaret Somerville, an ethicist from McGill University, notes that we live in exciting times, as we now have the science to support many of our teachings. While many have believed without seeing, some, like St. Thomas, need to see the connections. The truths we extract through our study of nature and science can reveal something about God, because scientific truth and religious truth lead us to God's truth.

The Vatican is made up of a number of congregations, commissions and academies dealing with Catholic education, governance, ecumenism and interreligous dialogue, among other key issues in our universal Church. One such academy, The Pontifical Academy of the Sciences, is dedicated to the dialogue between faith and the sciences.

The academy has a long and controversial history. It has its origins in Rome in 1603 under the patronage of Pope Clement VIII, with Galileo Galilei as the leader. It was dissolved after the death of its founder, but recreated by Pope Pius IX in 1847. In 1992, John Paul spoke on Galileo in an address to the academy, and in 1996 he addressed the academy on evolutionary theory. Galileo Galilei (1564–1642), an Italian scientist, was condemned by the Roman Inquisition in 1615 for his scientific discoveries. Because Galileo argued that the earth goes around the sun, the Inquisition found his views to be heretical; at the time, most people believed that all objects orbit the earth. While the Church has followed the logic of science in this matter for quite some time now, an apology to Galileo was issued by John Paul II. In an article, "The Galileo Affair," members of the Vatican Observatory explain John Paul II's interest in settling the controversy around Galileo:

Pope John Paul II named a commission to investigate again the Galileo affair; after the work of the Galileo commission was completed, Pope John Paul II's discourse to the Pontifical Academy of Science in 1992 stated that Galileo's sufferings at the hands of some individuals and church institutions were tragic and inescapable, and a consequence of a mutual incomprehension in those times between church theologians and the new scientists such as Galileo. To be clear, science as we know it was just being born and not even scientists of those times could comprehend fully what was happening. The Church officially apologized to Galileo in 2000.[80]

Since 1936, the Pontifical Academy of Sciences has been concerned with the study of scientific subjects in a variety of disciplines, in cooperation and dialogue with other disciplines. The Academy is an independent body within the Vatican and enjoys freedom of scientific research.

The Academy has as its goal the promotion of the progress of the mathematical, physical and natural sciences, and the study of related epistemological (nature of knowledge and understanding) questions and issues. The academy is a valuable source of objective scientific information that is made available to the Holy See and to the international scientific community.

The academy covers six main areas:

1. Fundamental science

2. The science and technology of global questions and issues

3. Science in favour of the problems of the Third World

4. The ethics and politics of science

5. Bioethics

6. Epistemology

It also covers nine scientific fields:

1. Physics

2. Astronomy

3. Chemistry

4. Earth and environment sciences

5. Life sciences (botany, agronomy, zoology, genetics, molecular biology, biochemistry, neurosciences, surgery)

6. Mathematics

7. Applied sciences

8. Philosophy

9. History of sciences

Members of the Academy, who are officially appointed by the pope, are elected and chosen from men and women of every race and religion, on the basis of their academic rigour and their high moral profile. Research has been conducted in the areas of adult stem cells, other areas in bioethics, genetically modified foods, the benefits of breastfeeding, and astrophysics, among many others. In 2014, the Academy is hosting a workshop entitled "Sustainable Humanity. Sustainable Nature."

The challenge for us today is to promote research that is life-giving. The National Catholic Bioethics Institute in the United States has produced an excellent DVD entitled *Cutting Through the Spin on Stem Cell Research and Cloning.* Father Tad Pacholczyk, the host and presenter, is both a scientist as well as a priest. He provides an excellent overview of the Church's ethical concerns about embryonic stem cell research and cloning. He also gives many examples of people being cured of a variety of ailments using adult stem cell research, while noting that no one has been saved using embryonic stem cells. The DVD, which is suitable for parish and home use, explores many of the questions concerned Catholics may have when it comes to ethical questions around these issues. He exposes the dark side of scientific research when God's laws are not honoured and respected. Canada has joined the discussion and has made numerous contributions in the area of bioethics awareness. The Canadian Catholic Bioethics Institute is a tremendous resource for Canadian Catholics. Staff of the Institute are available for diocesan/ parish presentations and have produced a number of helpful resources, including *Bioethics Matters* by Moira McQueen (Novalis, 2011).

In pursuing my interest in neuroscience and the newly emerging discipline of neurotheology, I have been intrigued by recent findings in the area of neuroplasticity and the benefits of faith and prayer. Dr. Andrew Newberg, Dr. Mario Beauregard and others have studied the impact of prayer and faith development on the brain. Dr. Beauregard studied the effect of mystical experience on the brains of Carmelite nuns:

> The main goal of this functional magnetic resonance imaging (fMRI) study was to identify the neural correlates of a mystical experience. The brain activity of Carmelite nuns was measured while they were subjectively in a state of union with God. This state was associated with significant loci of activation in the right medial orbitofrontal cortex, right middle temporal cortex, right inferior and superior parietal lobules, right caudate, left medial prefrontal cortex, left anterior cingulated cortex, left inferior parietal lobule, left insula, left caudate, and left brain stem. Other loci of activation were seen in the extrastriate visual cortex. These results suggest that mystical experiences are mediated by several brain regions and systems.[81]

While the language is very technical, it is clear that parts of the brain are activated with spiritual experience. This confirms the body, mind, spirit connection in the human person. In his book on neurotheology, a discipline that studies mind, brain and spirit connections, Dr. Andrew Newberg posits that neurotheology can lead to a deeper understanding of "the human brain and its associated capacity for responding to religious beliefs and having spiritual experiences."[82] Our mind can be made new after an encounter with Christ. We can learn to perceive correctly and experience the peace of Christ. Almost two thousand years ago, St. Paul encouraged us to put on the "mind of Christ" (1 Corinthians 2:16). St. Paul was on to something here regarding the correction of perception and thinking the thoughts of Jesus. Our minds need healing just as much as our bodies do. Paul did not need scientific research to prove the spiritual fruits of a life lived in Christ. An encounter with Christ does change us: our thoughts, our habits and our interactions with others. Today's research, for the doubting Thomases of the world, shows that an encounter with Christ bears fruit. Now the fruit can be seen in images!

Civic Life: Encountering Christ in Dialogue

"The emergence on the world stage of new economic, political and religious actors from the Islamic and Asian worlds has created an entirely new and unknown situation, rich in potential, but fraught with dangers and new temptations for dominion and power. Many responses have highlighted a variety of urgent situations in this sector, namely, a commitment to peace; the development and liberation of peoples; better international regulation and interaction of national governments; the search for possible areas of listening, coexistence, dialogue and collaboration between different cultures and religions; the defence of human rights and peoples, especially minorities; the promotion of the most vulnerable; and the integrity of creation and a commitment to the future of our planet." ∾ *INSTRUMENTUM LABORIS*, N. 57

The working document for the Synod on the New Evangelization emphasizes a "variety of urgent situations" that need to be addressed in this sector:

1. Commitment to Peace
Peace is a fruit of the Holy Spirit (Galatians 5:22). St. Paul says that if we do not live by the Holy Spirit, there will be enmities, strife, jealousy, anger, quarrels, dissensions and factions (Galatians 5:20). Peace in families and communities is possible only when two consenting parties agree to work out their difficulties with reason, faith and ethical approaches to conflict management. It is difficult to reconcile with an unwilling party. Encountering Christ involves encountering peace.

2. Liberation of Peoples
Pope John Paul II defined salvation as the deliverance from radical evil.[83]

To save is to liberate, heal and restore. Racism enslaves people; cultural discrimination enslaves people; unjust local and foreign policies enslave people; war enslaves; sexism enslaves; corruption enslaves. Jesus desires to liberate us from all that enslaves us. Access to education, health care and other resources empowers individuals to learn and grow into informed citizens. Men and women must work together to combat oppression and discrimination. Pope Francis, like Pope John Paul II, affirms women in leadership and has called for a "theology of women."

> I readily acknowledge that many women share pastoral responsibilities with priests, helping to guide people, families and groups offering new contributions to theological reflection. But we need to create still broader opportunities for a more incisive female presence in the Church. Because 'the feminine genius is needed in all expressions in the life of society, the presence of women must also be guaranteed in the workplace' and in the various other settings where important decisions are made, both in the Church and in social structures.
>
> ❧ POPE FRANCIS, *EVANGELII GAUDIUM*, N. 103

3. Regulation and Interaction of National Governments

The regulation of national governments has been explored in Catholic Social Teaching at several levels of magisterial teaching. In recent years, both Benedict XVI and the Pontifical Council for Justice and Peace (PCJP) focused on the need to promote freedom, subsidiarity and non-coercion when it comes to nations working with other nations on world authority. A PCJP document entitled "Reforming the International and Financial Monetary Systems" created an uproar: "In fact, one can see an emerging requirement for a body that will carry out the functions of a kind of 'central world bank' that regulates the flow and system of monetary exchanges as do the national central banks."[84] Here's another one:

> Of course, this transformation will be made at the cost of a gradual, balanced transfer of a part of each nation's powers to a world authority and to regional authorities, but this is necessary at a time when

the dynamism of human society and the economy and the progress of technology are transcending borders, which are in fact already very eroded in a globalized world.[85]

So explosive were the reactions to these and other statements in the document that Cardinal Tarcisio Bertone, Secretary of State at the time, rejected it and said that all documents had to be vetted by him before publication.[86]

As extreme as these statements are, similar ones are found elsewhere. While Pope Benedict XVI called for "a true world political authority," "vested with the effective power to ensure for all, regard for justice, and respect for rights,"[87] he placed more emphasis on the conversion of hearts and minds. These statements challenge us to think about national and global authority. Some propose more diversification and autonomy, protecting nationalistic rights and remaining distinct. The proposal made by Benedict XVI and the PCJP require individuals of great ethical stature and maturity. Is it realistic to propose such an agenda when leadership is in need of ongoing conversion? Christ can be encountered only where there is justice and truth.

Pope Francis was quick to address this crisis in justice and the regulation of banks. On May 16, 2013, he delivered his first major speech on the financial crisis, calling for the end of the "cult of money" and declaring that "money has to serve, not to rule." He urged ethical financial reforms driven by "person centered ethics." He denounced "the cult of money and the dictatorship of an economy which is faceless and lacking any truly humane goal." Two days later, in his address to members of a variety of lay ecclesial movements, he said, "people are dying of hunger because of the crisis but all we talk about is the banks." Pope Francis has been very clear and critical of the current banking situation. If policies are not changing, those in positions of leadership have not been changed themselves. At the end of June 2013, he announced a new committee to oversee the reform of the Institute of Works, also know as the Vatican Bank.

I beg the Lord to grant us more politicians who are genuinely disturbed by the state of society, the people, the lives of the poor! It is vital that government leaders and financial leaders take heed and broaden their horizons, working to ensure that all citizens have dignified work, education and healthcare. Why not turn to God and ask him to inspire their plans. ∾ POPE FRANCIS, *EVANGELII GAUDIUM*, N. 205

4. Dialogue between different cultures and religions

Muslims and Christians together make up over half the world's population. Without peace and justice between these two religious communities, there can be no meaningful peace in the world. The future of the world depends on peace between Muslims and Christians. (*A Common Word*, 2007)[88]

The Catholic Church has initiated official dialogues with various Christian traditions and world religions at the universal, national and local levels. An Internet search for the Pontifical Council for Interreligious Dialogue and the Pontifical Council for Promoting Christian Unity will reveal the numerous dialogues that have been enriched and supported for several decades. Theologians and other experts have been appointed to these dialogues to speak for their bishops and communicate the fruits and challenges of local dialogues. The Church supports four levels of dialogue with members of other faiths, such as Muslims:

- Dialogue of Life (sharing of resources around family issues, etc.)

- Dialogue of Theological Exchange (Seminars exploring views on creation, sin, etc.)

- Dialogue of Action (social justice projects)

- Dialogue of Religious Experience (sharing the fruit of faith and prayer)[89]

Dialogue is not about proselytizing. Instead, it gives us an opportunity to witness to and share the fruits of our faith journey. It is our duty to share our joy and faith in Jesus Christ.

> "Evangelization and interreligious dialogue, far from being opposed,
> mutually support and nourish one another."
> ◌ POPE FRANCIS, *EVANGELII GAUDIUM*, N. 251

5. Defence of Human Rights and Peoples: Ethnic Minorities and the Most Vulnerable

Catholic Social Teaching affirms the dignity of all people, created in the image and likeness of God. In *Dignitatis Humanae* (1965), the Second Vatican Council affirmed religious freedom, which is the right to pursue religious truth without the fear of persecution or discrimination. Too often we hear of the violation of human rights, where the dignity of the person is not respected or even considered. Lately, both Muslims and Christians have experienced increased discrimination and persecution due to the sins of the few. Muslims in the West may fear discrimination due to the acts of extremists in their own faith tradition. Muslims in the East, meanwhile, have experienced devastation and war. Christians in the East fear persecution and violence and have fled the region due to attacks on their communities. According to *The Economist*, up to two thirds of Iraq's 1.5 million Christians are thought to have emigrated in the past ten years.[90] Moreover, in certain countries, such as Saudi Arabia and North Korea, some Christians are not free to practice their faith in public. In these countries, "violent opposition to Christianity forces Christians to hide their faith in their own beloved homeland" (Pope Francis, EG, n. 86).

In 2013 in Quebec, French Canadians are debating the right for government employees to wear religious articles. A proposed bill, the Charter of Values, would prohibit public sector employees from wearing religious symbols. This means a Catholic nun who is a teacher or hospital social worker may not be allowed to wear her habit or a crucifix. This means that members of other faiths will be prohibited from wearing symbols of their faith as well. Such a proposed bill should trouble all people of faith. It will set a dangerous precedent for other provinces or states. Religious freedom, the church teaches, is a "fundamental human right" (EG, n. 255).

Other forms of discrimination have led to the oppression of ethnic minorities, the exploitation of the elderly, and the complete abolition of the rights of the unborn. To be pro-life means to protect the sanctity of life from conception through to natural death. As the proverb says, "The road to hell is paved with good intentions." Catholics are called to be informed and mindful of the Church's social teaching. What some may present as a good intention can open the door to atrocity, supporting what Pope John Paul II called the culture of death (see *Evangelium Vitae*). We encounter Christ in the care and protection of the unborn and the vulnerable.

6. Integrity of Creation and a Commitment to the Future of Our Planet

"My dear friends, God's creation is one and it is good. The concerns for nonviolence, sustainable development, justice and peace, and care for our environment are of vital importance for humanity. They cannot, however, be understood apart from a profound reflection on the innate dignity of every human life from conception to natural death: a dignity conferred by God himself and thus inviolable." ❧ POPE BENEDICT XVI, ADDRESS, WELCOMING CELEBRATION BY YOUNG PEOPLE FOR WORLD YOUTH DAY IN SYDNEY, AUSTRALIA, JULY 17, 2008

Pope John Paul II's groundbreaking 1990 World Day of Peace message, *Peace with God the Creator, Peace with All of Creation*, inspired conferences of bishops around the world to respond to the needs of people and the environment:

> Faced with the widespread destruction of the environment, people everywhere are coming to understand that we cannot continue to use the goods of the earth as we have in the past. The public in general as well as political leaders are concerned about this problem, and experts from a wide range of disciplines are studying its causes. Moreover, a new *ecological awareness* is beginning to emerge which, rather than being downplayed, ought to be encouraged to develop into concrete programmes and initiatives. (n. 1)

The US Conference of Catholic Bishops released its first statement on the environment, *Renewing the Earth: An Invitation to Reflection and Action on Environment in Light of Catholic Social Teaching*, and in 1993 created the Environmental Justice Program. These documents and programs call for a deepened respect for God's creation, and address the ethical dimensions of the environmental crisis and how it impacts the poor, the land and the earth's resources.

"The Church is likewise conscious of the responsibility which all of us have for our world, for the whole of creation, which we must love and respect." ∿ POPE FRANCIS, MARCH 20, 2013, ADDRESS TO REPRESENTATIVES OF CHURCHES, ECCLESIAL COMMUNITIES, AND MEMBERS OF OTHER FAITHS

On April 8, 2013, the Episcopal Commission for Justice and Peace of the Canadian Conference of Catholic Bishops released a statement on the environment: *Building a New Culture: Central Themes in Recent Church Teaching on the Environment*. The commission draws attention to eight central themes:[91]

1. Human Beings are Creatures Made in God's Image

2. Creation has an Intrinsic Order

3. "Human Ecology" and its Relationship to Environmental Ecology

4. Responsible Stewardship

5. Care for the Environment is a Moral Issue

6. Solidarity

7. Creation and Spirituality

8. Responses to Current Environmental Problems consisting of:

   » Urgent need for action

   » Policy development

   » International cooperation

» Financial responsibility

» Lowering consumption

How do we encounter Christ in this sector? By caring for his people, finding and using helpful resources, and caring for God's creation.

Media and Social Communications: Encountering Christ in Life-giving Media

The Catholic Church was founded by Christ our Lord to bring salvation to all people. It feels obliged, therefore, to preach the gospel. In the same way, it believes that its task involves employing the means of social communication to announce the good news of salvation and teach people how to use them properly. (Decree on the Means of Social Communication, *Inter Mirifica*, 1963, n. 3)

Pope Paul VI emphasized the need for "proper means and language" for re-proposing Christ to all people (*Evangelii Nuntiandi*, nn. 46, 56). The working document for the synod on the New Evangelization insists on the necessity of devising "new tools and new expressions" to ensure that the gospel be better communicated (*Instrumentum Laboris*, n. 8).

In his book *The Emerging Millennials*, Reginald Bibby, a sociologist of religion, says that the Internet is the playground for the new generation.[92] Father Tom Lynch, Canadian director for Priests for Life, once said, "Why should the devil use all the best technology?"[93]It is easy to see how media and social communications have been used and exploited to disfigure humanity and desensitize minds. If sin corrupts, grace can perfect! The Church needs faith-filled, skilled technicians and media savvy individuals to speak for the Church and create resources using various platforms and formats, including social media, that feed and inspire people. Father Robert Barron's *Word on Fire* has been a huge success, as he has reached millions with his website and other communications resources. Eternal Word Television Network (EWTN) in the US and Salt and Light Television in Canada have reached many people in their homes as well. Apart from these initiatives, it would be great to see dioceses come together to buy time on more mainstream networks to reach the unconverted:

> It would be shameful if by their inactivity Catholics allowed the word of God to be silenced or obstructed by the technical difficulties which these media present and by their admittedly enormous cost. For this reason the Council reminds them that they have *the obligation to sustain and assist Catholic newspapers, periodicals, film-projects, radio and television stations and programs....* (Decree on the Means of Social Communication, n. 17)

I am the host of a weekly radio show on AM 530, Radio Teopoli (Canada), a Catholic station that broadcasts in English and Italian. My show is dedicated to the New Evangelization. Some of the shows cover an overview of various doctrines, while others include guest interviews on a variety of topics. Some guests have shared vocation stories and other stories of conversion. We use a variety of music that appeals to all ages. The music is not always explicitly Catholic in content, as there are many songs with lyrics that speak of love and forgiveness. People are attracted to people of faith who understand the culture.

Pope Paul VI said that communicators are obliged to pay continual attention to and to carry on an uninterrupted observation of the external world: "You must continually stand at the window, open to the world; you are obliged to study the facts, the events, the opinions, the current interest, the thought of the surrounding environment."[94] It is wise to develop a roster of identified media spokespersons who are trained in a variety of disciplines and who know the language of the Church, and to coordinate media training where applicable. It would be helpful, for example, to provide a training day for Catholic students of broadcast journalism to cover the following areas:

• Church language (e.g., "What is the Curia?")

• Apologetics (explaining and defending the teachings, beliefs and practices of the faith)

• Responses to hot-button issues (e.g., assisted suicide, stem cell research, in vitro fertilization)

Diocesan communications personnel can work to nurture and develop relationships with local media to enhance the public image of the Church. For example, the Communications Director for the Archdiocese of Toronto created a "voices" database with over 30 individuals who assisted him with the papal conclave in 2013.

> "The Church would feel guilty before the Lord if she did not utilize these powerful means that human skill is daily rendering more perfect ... In them she finds a modern and effective version of the pulpit. Thanks to them she succeeds in speaking to the multitudes."
>
> ∾ POPE PAUL VI, *EVANGELII NUNTIANDI*, N. 45

Many dioceses throughout the world have some sort of plan to use communications – print, audio, video, in both traditional and digital formats – to share the gospel message. The following two goals should guide our efforts in this area.

1. Strive for Personal Holiness: Seeing Salvation

With so many people using social media on a daily basis, it would be wise to use some of these outlets to propose holiness or transformation. Someone may be more apt to watch a brief YouTube video than go out and buy a book on the call to holiness. Some people are able to use their home computers to produce short amateur videos. It would be wonderful to see videos of "before and after" transformations. These videos, which would include personal testimonies and stories of conversion, would give viewers the visual of the being made new that comes with encountering Christ. People need to see salvation. While books and other print media help to communicate this message, seeing the transformation through pictures and video would be outstanding. Diocesan Communications guidelines for sharing conversion stories could be developed to help producers and those sharing testimonials. Jesus was a master communicator, as was St. Paul. Are we exploring all of the opportunities available to us? Pope Francis says we cannot "be content with a desk-bound theology" (EG, n. 133).

> Christ commanded the apostles and their successors to "teach all nations," to be "the light of the world," and to announce the Good News in all places and at all times. During his life on earth, Christ showed

himself to be the perfect Communicator, while the Apostles used what means of social communication were available in their time. It is now necessary that the same message be carried by the means of social communication that are available today. *Indeed, it would be difficult to suggest that Christ's command was being obeyed unless all the opportunities offered by the modern media to extend to vast numbers of people the announcement of his Good News were being used.* (Pastoral Instruction on the Means of Social Communication, n. 126)

2. Proclaim the Gospel in the Language of the People

While our teachings are rich and profound, we should communicate in the language of the people and be mindful of the various learning needs and language barriers that may prevent evangelization and proper catechesis. We need evangelization and catechesis that is both accessible and comprehensible. Pope Francis calls for preaching that is simple, clear and organized (EG, n. 158).

The message of Pope Benedict XVI for the 41st World Communications Day states:

> The Church herself, in light of the message of salvation entrusted to her, is also a teacher of humanity and welcomes the opportunity to offer assistance to parents, educators, communicators, and young people. *Her own parish and school programs should be in the forefront of media education today.* Above all, the Church desires to share a vision of human dignity that is central to all worthy human communication. "Seeing with the eyes of Christ, I can give to others much more than their outward necessities; I can give them the look of love which they crave" (*Deus Caritas Est*, n. 18) (n. 4)

How do we encounter Christ in this sector? We see his image in those who communicate his will through social media and communications. We are fed by this communication, not disfigured. If we are not careful, Jesus will remain hidden in the technical language we use.

Religion: Encountering Christ in Catechesis and Faith Development

In his homily of April 17, 2013, Pope Francis used the image of a babysitter to describe how some may view the Church. He cautioned that the Church cannot be reduced to "a babysitter who takes care of the child just to get him to sleep." This approach, he said, would make the Church a "slumbering church." The way to avoid this, he continues, is for members of the Church to remember their baptism and to go out and evangelize. "When we do this the Church becomes a mother who generates children," proclaiming Christ with "our life, our testimony and even with our words."

> "Many lament the excessive bureaucratic character of ecclesiastical structures, perceived as far removed from the average person and his everyday concerns, which causes a reduction in the dynamism of ecclesial communities, the loss of enthusiasm at its roots and a decline in missionary zeal." ⚭ *INSTRUMENTUM LABORIS*, N. 69

How do we encourage and inspire a "spiritual reawakening" and "reanimation" of baptized Catholics? The authors of the working document are aware that other groups may be attracting our members using "aggressive, proselytizing methods" (n. 66) and tactics that promise prosperity and success in life. The authors caution that we are not to imitate these methods. Instead, we are to work toward "giving individuals a sense of meaning in their lives" (n. 66).

Jesus gives individuals a sense of meaning in their lives; everyone has the right to hear this message (n. 33). We need to offer an adequate response to the needs of individuals, following the signs of the times. It is through our culture that we reveal our identity and what gives meaning to our lives. But we must remember that the New Evangelization begins with "me." I must consider this question: "What do I need to do, think and say to be a credible witness, another Christ?" Once my own spiritual house is in order, or at least as close as possible, my witness and words can offer a foretaste of restoration to others, a kind of "forestate" of salvation. Just before the Ascension in Luke's Gospel

(24:47), Jesus instructs his disciples to go out to baptize and evangelize. The key, according to Jesus, is to start in Jerusalem (the home base of the apostles): start at home, then go out to the world. When I myself am satisfied, I can feed others from the surplus of love that fills my heart. Jesus, who is always the same, forms us into a new creation. The "New You" is at the heart of the New Evangelization.

CATECHESIS

Jesus is at the heart of catechesis (*Catechism of the Catholic Church*, n. 426). If someone does not encounter Jesus as a person in the Catholic curriculum, he or she will not be changed. If the gospel is not presented in a way that is accessible or comprehensible, the student will not discover Jesus. The following is the opening prayer from the preface of the Roman Catechism, the first major Catechism from the Council of Trent:

> Whoever teaches must become "all things to all men" (1 Cor. 22), to win everyone to Christ ... Above all, teachers must not imagine that a single kind of soul has been entrusted to them, and that consequently it is lawful to teach and form equally all the faithful in true piety with one and the same method! Let them realize that some are in Christ as newborn babes, others as adolescents, and still others as adults in full command of their powers ... Those who are called to the ministry of preaching must suit their words to the maturity and understanding of their hearers, as they hand on the teaching of the mysteries of faith and the rules of moral conduct.

The key words here are "those who are called to the ministry of preaching" – and I would add teaching – "must suit their words to the maturity and understanding of their hearers." We cannot teach and form all people using the same methods and language. Language in our Catholic tradition can alienate as well as feed; Jesus becomes hiddenly present in some texts. It can feed those with a certain intellect and training, while alienating and discouraging others. It may even turn them off the gospel message.

We need to look at our language and methods of communication so that new methods and approaches can be used in all levels of faith formation when needed. One of the students in my Christology class once told me that he was talking about Jesus with a resident in a health care facility. This student was eager to share some of his new-found knowledge about Jesus. As he began to share his thoughts on the pre-existent Word of God, the eyes of the resident glazed over and he almost fell asleep. My student learned very quickly that he had to switch gears and use different language in his sharing about Christ. This is something I need to work on as well. We may take our knowledge for granted and assume that others are familiar with the language of theology.

Retention of content is another problem. My friend Anne once told me that she got 97% in Grade 13 Calculus but could not say anything now about what she learned. As the saying goes, "Use it or lose it." Dr. Norman Doidge, in his book *The Brain that Changes Itself*, explores the dynamics of neuroplasticity. The brain, he says, has to keep working, perhaps as hard as it did while learning a language or a musical instrument. Catechesis is no different from other disciplines in this way. A child may receive wonderful catechetical instruction by a faith-filled teacher, but unless she continues to use it or study it, she may not retain the content. On the other hand, many seniors who memorized parts of the Baltimore Catechism know who made them, but they may not be practising their faith.

Problem-based learning is an approach that encourages ownership of the material to be learned. Children remember researching saints in preparation for Confirmation. University students remember their research papers. This is why teachers make great contestants for trivia shows. They come to own their material because they use it on a regular basis. While some people may remember material they helped to prepare, other people will remember the content of our faith that speaks to their hearts. They may not remember all of the official Church teaching cited in this book, but they may remember the story about my friend who missed being known by her mother. This story may have triggered an insight into God's love for us. God knows us and loves us with great intimacy. Some may take away some of the facts shared in the section on demographics, while others will remember Howard Storm's near-death experience or the fireman who was given a sneak preview of his restored self. These stories touch the heart and reveal God's love. God wants to introduce us to our true selves through the work of Jesus Christ.

Faith is a lived experience that requires nurturing and time. It also involves trusting other Christians and fellowship. Catechesis alone is not enough to facilitate an encounter with Christ. Change or transformation indicates a person's intimate knowledge of Christ. If the intimacy is not there, catechism or religious instruction is reduced to just another discipline that will be forgotten if it is not used and internalized. You know a person has encountered Christ if you detect change for the better. Catechesis, according to Pope John Paul II, should encourage students to know Christ:

> To put it more precisely: within the whole process of evangelization, the aim of catechesis is to be the teaching and maturation stage, that is to say, the period in which the Christian, having accepted by faith the person of Jesus Christ as the one Lord and having given Him complete adherence by sincere conversion of heart, endeavors to know better this Jesus to whom he has entrusted himself: to know His "mystery," the kingdom of God proclaimed by Him, the requirements and promises contained in His Gospel message, and the paths that He has laid down for anyone who wishes to follow Him ... In his closing speech at the fourth general assembly of the synod, Pope Paul VI rejoiced "to see how everyone drew attention to the absolute need for systematic catechesis, precisely because it is this reflective study of the Christian mystery that fundamentally distinguishes catechesis from all other ways of presenting the word of God." (n. 50) (*Catechesi Tradendae*, n. 20, 21)

In view of practical difficulties, attention must be drawn to some of the characteristics of this instruction:

- It must be systematic, not improvised but programmed to reach a precise goal.

- It must deal with essentials, without any claim to tackle all disputed questions or to transform itself into theological research or scientific exegesis.

- It must nevertheless be sufficiently complete, not stopping short at the initial proclamation of the Christian mystery, such as we have in the *kerygma*.

- It must be an integral Christian initiation, open to all the other factors of Christian life.

Pope John Paul II said that being a Christian involves surrendering to the Word of God and knowing the profound meaning of that Word. (*Catechesi Tradendae*, n. 20)

Mass attendance is another hot-button issue. The US Conference of Catholic Bishops offers the following reasons for decline in mass attendance:

> Most Catholics stop attending Mass because they (1) have busy schedules or a lack of time, (2) have family responsibilities, (3) have health problems or disabilities, (4) have conflicts with work, (5) do not believe missing Mass is a sin, or (6) believe that they are not very religious people. (USCCB Committee on Evangelization and Catechesis, *Disciples Called to Witness: The New Evangelization*)

It is a shame that many Catholics are missing out on being fed in so many ways. They miss out on the Eucharist, being fed by the Body of Christ. They miss out on fellowship and being fed by the spiritual gifts of others. When my eldest daughter began living on her own, we realized it was important to stay connected regularly. We speak or send text messages every day, but above all we make a point to meet at least once a week for a meal. I could tell her I love her every day over the phone, but this does not have the same effect as seeing her in person. The same is true for our participation in the Eucharist. By participating in Sunday Eucharist, we show that we need God and others in our spiritual journey. When we pray the Prayer of the Faithful together, we show our fellow parishioners that we are here for them. They can count on our prayers and support and vice versa.

In his book *Cornerstones of Faith: Reconciliation, Eucharist and Stewardship*, Cardinal Thomas Collins underscores the importance of the Eucharist. Just as schoolchildren cannot focus and learn when they are hungry, we cannot manage day-to-day struggles when we are spiritually malnourished. After we are fed, we are sent forth to proclaim the gospel. Jesus fed the crowd with food before he fed them with words. They were able to focus and receive instruction after they were satisfied. We cannot feed others if we are running on empty.

GOD'S CURRICULUM

Apart from catechesis, another form of curriculum focuses on the inner life of the person. The short yet insightful Second Letter of Peter provides an excellent curriculum for the Christian life. In one of the very first verses (1:4), Peter shares that we can be "participants of the divine nature." This is one of the reasons why the Word became flesh: Jesus became one of us so we can be like him. The key is to be like God with God's assistance, creature and Creator working together. We evangelize to proclaim this mystery: Christ came to reveal our true selves to us and show us the way to this new creation. We can participate in his humanity and divinity. Jesus is the link back to God, back to what was lost and so much more.

But this amazing mystery is not well communicated. When we gather to celebrate the Liturgy of the Eucharist, at the preparation of the gifts, the priest *quietly* (inaudibly) says:

> By the mystery of this water and wine
> may we come to share in the divinity of Christ
> who humbled himself to share in our humanity.

The oldest known version of this prayer is a Collect for the Nativity of Our Lord from the Leonine Sacramentary, dating back to the seventh century:

> O God, who wonderfully created the dignity of man's nature, and have more wonderfully renewed it, grant, we beseech you, that we may be made partakers of His divinity who humbled himself to become a partaker of our humanity, Christ Your Son.

And here is the prayer from the Extraordinary Form of the Mass:

> O God, who wonderfully created the dignity of man's nature, and have more wonderfully renewed it, grant that, through the mystery of this water and wine, we may be made partakers of His divinity who humbled himself to become a partaker of our humanity, Jesus Christ, Your Son ...

This prayer is deeply rooted in scripture: 2 Maccabees 15:39, John 19:34, Romans 5:2, 2 Peter 1:4 and Philippians 2:8. Scripture and Tradition confirm this truth: **Jesus came to be one of us so we can be like him**. Depending on how much your pastor projects when he says this prayer during Mass, you may never hear it! Many Catholics are amazed when I draw attention to it and to the deeper meaning of this prayer. Pope John Paul II spoke of this mystery often:

> All who commit themselves to following Christ are given the fullness of life: the divine image is restored, renewed and brought to perfection in them. God's plan for human beings is this, that they should be "conformed to the image of his Son" (Rm. 8:29). Only thus, in the splendour of this image, can man be freed from the slavery of idolatry, rebuild lost fellowship and rediscover his true identity. (*Evangelium Vitae*, n. 36)

In his second letter, Peter tells us that this is a possibility, then goes on to share how we can arrive at this point. He says the following qualities will keep us "from being ineffective and unfruitful in the knowledge of our Lord Jesus Christ" (2 Peter 1:8):

• Goodness

• Knowledge

• Self-control

• Endurance

• Godliness

• Mutual affection

• Love

He concludes his letter by telling us that all of this is ours! There is no need to be "barren in the knowledge of God." It is not limited to the intellectual giants of our tradition. Self-knowledge, humility and love open our hearts and minds to the glory of God. This is the knowledge we retain. Once we have this type of knowledge, the content of any catechesis can be understood and internalized – not just memorized (at best) or forgotten. The more full we are of God's love and knowledge, the more able we will be to feed and inspire others. An interested heart will be attracted to the external curriculum of our faith.

The external curriculum of our faith builds on the internal, spiritual curriculum of God. We start with the desire and humility we need to know ourselves. What shaped my personality? Genes? Prenatal or post-natal stress? Calm or chaos in the family? Ethnicity? Loss? Betrayal? How have I responded to this? Have I responded to God's desire to make me new? Do parts of my personality need healing and restoration? Are any of my habits and thoughts not life-giving?

The Church encourages us to be humble and to know when to give and when to wait on the Lord so that we can be full and overflowing with graces and wisdom. Jesus can be reproduced in us if we take the time to be open to this life-giving challenge.

> "The real newness is the newness which God himself mysteriously brings about and inspires, provokes, guides and accompanies us in a thousand ways. The life of the Church should always reveal clearly that God takes the initiative, that 'he loved us first' (1 Jn. 4:19) and that he alone 'gives the growth' (1 Cor. 3: 7). This conviction enables us to maintain a spirit of joy in the midst of a task so demanding and challenging that it engages our entire life. God asks everything of us, yet at the same time he offers everything to us."
>
> ᘉ POPE FRANCIS, *EVANGELII GAUDIUM*, N. 12

7

Mary, the Star of
the New Evangelization

Salvation came to us from the " yes" uttered by a lowly maiden from a small town on the fringes of a great empire.

∽ POPE FRANCIS, *EVANGELII GAUDIUM*, N. 197

Pope John Paul II referred to Mary as "the Star of the New Evangelization" (*Ecclesia in America*, n. 11). In a homily on October 7, 2012, Pope Benedict XVI continued this tradition by entrusting the synod's work to Mary, the star of the New Evangelization. The outpouring of the Holy Spirit, he said, will guide us. Just as a star is light and brilliance, Mary, our star, leads the way to Jesus and the gospel message. The Holy Spirit worked through her and inspired her own mission, to be the first disciple, the mother of Jesus. Without her, Pope Francis declares, "we could never truly understand the spirit of the new evangelization" (EG, n. 284). The words of the Angel Gabriel in Luke's gospel (Luke 1:26-38) shed light on this mystery and inspire our own journey.

Greetings, favoured one! The Lord is with you.

Even before her mission is revealed, Mary is reminded that she is not alone. Feeling alone can discourage individuals and prevent them from moving forward, from trusting God and others.

Do not be afraid, Mary, for you have found favour with God.

Baptism makes us sons and daughters of God. We are God's children and he knows us with a deep intimacy. Knowing we are known and loved encourages trust and fellowship. Mary knows she is not alone, but she may be confused, not knowing what this encounter is all about. She is told not to be afraid. Pope John Paul II, in his inaugural homily, told the crowd, "Do not be afraid!" Fear is not of God; it is not a fruit of the Holy Spirit. Fear agitates and prevents growth and flourishing. Fear keeps us from saying yes. John Paul II went on to say that "Jesus takes away nothing" but "gives us everything." By "nothing," I believe he was referring to those habits and thoughts that are not life-giving; if we are purified of these, we did not need them in the first place. They do not help us to grow and experience God's love. The "everything" consists of the love, humility and joy we need to experience communion with God and with each other. We will be given all of the gifts and blessings we need to become another Christ. As Peter says, these are our gifts; there is no barrenness in life in Christ (2 Peter 1:8). Mary's yes to God's plan was needed so that Jesus could become one of us.

And now, you will conceive in your womb and bear a son, and you will name him Jesus. He will be great, and will be called Son of the Most High, and the Lord God will give to him the throne of his ancestor David. He will reign over the house of Jacob forever, and of his kingdom there will be no end.

Jesus' name – which means "God's salvation" – reveals his mission. Mary will conceive the Son of God in her womb with the power of the Holy Spirit. This same Spirit makes us another Christ, but there is a process involved. Mary was preserved free from the stain of original sin and personal sin. We, on the other hand, need to be open to the process of transformation and sanctification. Slowly but surely, grace and the Holy Spirit will work with our human nature and restore that which has been disfigured through pride, selfishness, impatience, and so on. We experience a softening of our characters, and this humility allows the

Holy Spirit to work on our minds, thoughts and habits. We, too, can give birth to Christ in our lives! The less we sin, the more visible Christ is in us.

The Holy Spirit will come upon you, and the power of the Most High will overshadow you; therefore the child to be born will be holy; he will be called Son of God ...

When the Holy Spirit descends on us, we are anointed and protected. The presence of the Holy Spirit transforms us, purifies us and makes us holy.

For nothing will be impossible with God

These words appear soon after the Angel Gabriel tells Mary that her cousin Elizabeth has conceived a son in her old age. God has done the impossible with both Mary and Elizabeth. We can get caught up in our wounds, our past, our mistakes, our family drama, our workplace drama, and be discouraged. Discouragement can lead to despair, and a vicious cycle begins. Here is a story, author unknown, that has been widely circulated on the topic of despair and discouragement:

> The devil decided to go out of business, so he put all the instruments of his business on sale. There was anger, lust, greed, jealousy, passion for wealth, ego – he put up everything for sale, and people bought them all. But then somebody noticed that he still had something in his bag. So they asked him, "What is it that you have got?" The devil said, "These are my most effective tools. I am not putting these up for sale, just in case I decide to get back into business. And above all, even if I put them on sale, they will be too expensive, as they are the best instruments of my work to somehow destroy life."

People asked, "Tell us what they are!"

The devil said, "Discouragement and despair."

Mary hoped in God's providence. She witnessed the impossible many times in her life – the incarnation and the resurrection, to name two. Hope is the remedy where there is fear and discouragement. Discouragement is not a fruit of the Holy Spirit. God does not desire that we be agitated or worried, because he created us for joy and hope. The next time you are tempted to despair or are agitated, know that this is not of God. Pray to be released from this falsehood and to feel truth, the language of the

135

Holy Spirit. Mary was a woman of hope and modelled perseverance and faithfulness even when things were falling apart. She was inspired by the Holy Spirit and encouraged in times of struggle and bitterness. Even though she was conceived without the stain of original sin, she was not exempt from pain and suffering. She had to drink from a number of bitter cups: Joseph's doubt regarding her pregnancy, the flight to Egypt, the child Jesus missing for three days, public gossip and slander about herself and her Son, threats against her Son, and finally his crucifixion. How did she survive these struggles? How did she continue to trust in the goodness of God? The resurrection of Jesus reminded her of God's supremacy and goodness. God restored her Son, gave him a glorified body and gave him back to her and the world through his love. The resurrection reminded her that loss and death are not the final word, because God's love vindicates and redeems. She is a model of hope and resilience.

Pope Francis says that there is a "Marian 'style'" to the Church's work of evangelization (EG, n. 288). This means that love and tenderness can conquer hearts. "Contemplating Mary, we realize that she who praised God for 'bringing down the mighty from their thrones' and 'sending the rich away empty' (Lk. 1:52-53) is also the one who brings homely warmth to our pursuit of justice" (EG, n. 288). Mary is a model of evangelization because of her approach to life. She is active, tender and contemplative, and ponders the mysteries of God in her heart. She gave birth to Christ over 2,000 years ago, and we are called to give birth to Christ in our communities.

Consider the following reflection on hope whenever you are tempted to doubt God's plan for you:

OBSTACLES TO HOPE (NOT FRUITS OF THE HOLY SPIRIT)

> "Let your heart not be troubled ... Am I not here, I who am your Mother?"
> ◯ᴗ MARY'S WORDS TO JUAN DIEGO: NICAN MOPOHUA, LINES 118–119

1. **Fear:** "Perfect love casts out fear" (1 John 4:18) and perfect fear casts out love. Past pain makes us paranoid when we worry about the past repeating itself. Some call this evil foreboding. It

traps us in an unknown future and paralyzes us with thoughts that are not true. Take the time to investigate and examine your thoughts. How do I know this is true? Am I reasoning?

2. **Shame:** Past sins that are not confessed can wound us and can go on to haunt us. God's love, mercy and forgiveness are greater than any wound. Don't allow wounds to become gods in your life. Meditate on the parable of the Prodigal Son (Luke 15) and see how the father does not shame the son with his past. The father is content with the son's contrition. God blesses humility with peace and restoration. We may prevent this healing and restoration from taking place in another individual if we continually shame them and remind them of their past. This may delay their healing and compound existing shame. Be like the father in the prodigal son story and trust that perfect contrition shows that one is ready for a new life. Give the other person the chance to move on. The path to contrition is purification in and of itself.

3. **Negative Thinking:** There is a proverb: "Like a dog returns to his vomit, a fool returns to his folly" (Proverbs 26:11). Negative thinking is very seductive; it hardens our hearts, makes us critical and disfigures the likeness of God in us. It sets us back, ages us and, according to authors Patricia Treece and Dr. Bill Webster, may even hurt our immune system.

4. **Pride:** The three temptations of Christ come to mind in the consideration of pride. In Matthew's account (Matthew 4:1-11) the order in which the temptations appear is not arbitrary: hunger, despair and the desire to tempt God with it, and finally pride. The attachment to status, the desire to compromise one's integrity in order to achieve status and titles, and overall focus on the self and advancement can only serve to disfigure and deform the person. Pride serves the self, not God.

5. **Impatience:** Impatience and restlessness tempt us to not trust God's will or plan for our lives. In this case, our prayer should

include the request for peace in our waiting. When we are not open to understanding God's will, sometimes when we want justice, what we really want is revenge. That's not how God works: it's all about restoration of original and authentic justice and freedom. There is more satisfaction when we know someone is contrite and understands what he has done. This is why Jesus commands us to love and pray for our enemies (Matthew 5:43-48). We pray for them because we want them to understand their actions. Understanding leads to a healthy remorse and healing. A humble remorse will prevent self-loathing. This will lead to their own redemption and reconciliation with others.

6. **Lack of preparedness:** We are not reading the signs of the times and the types of seasons we experience as individuals, communities and nations. While we should not be obsessive or paranoid, we should not buy into a naïve optimism, where this is no rational reflection on the signs of the times and the need to prepare for a dramatic shift in seasons: health, finance, relationships, community disaster, and so on.

7. **Not praying through the struggle:** Despair is the opposite of hope because it seduces us into thinking that there is no hope for our future. Prayer feeds and sustains us in good times and in bad. In seasons of plenty, it keeps us thankful. In seasons of drought, it gives us hope.

HELPS TO HOPE (ALL OF THIS INVOLVES PRAYER AND SOMETIMES FASTING)

1. **Patience:** This involves waiting it out without being spiritually or emotionally passive. We pray for the grace and strength to cooperate with God's will. God will show us when to act or when to take a detour. This may require prayer coupled with fasting.

2. **Self-awareness**: Self-knowledge gives us an insight into habits that are not life-giving: How have I contributed to this situation?

Why am I jealous? Why do I get angry? If I have self-knowledge, I will know what to bring to prayer.

3. **Preparedness:** Should I be preparing in some way – money, food, material and spiritual blessings – building stamina so that I may be ready for a dramatic shift in seasons? This involves a wise optimism concerning the future.

4. **Radical Trust:** This involves trusting God's will. Faith involves belief, knowledge and trust. The first time we are called to trust God may be the most difficult. Once we experience God's faithfulness, even if there is loss, and survive the struggle, it may be easier to trust the next time we are faced with a challenge.

5. **Humility:** This involves surrendering past hurts and being open to seeing yourself as God sees you. Do you believe that God can redeem your losses?

6. **Positive attitude:** Do you believe God will protect your heart? Do you believe God will walk with you during good times and bad? Approach God at all times, like a loving parent. Patricia Treece and Andrew Newberg report that positive thinking is good for the brain.

7. **Gratitude:** Before the miracle of the multiplication of the loaves and fishes (Matthew 15:32-39), Jesus thanked God. He was aware of the need of the crowd and did not despair. If we can learn to thank God even when there is little, we will continue to thank God when there are bigger blessings. We build spiritual muscle with gratitude.

Mary, through her intercessory prayers, inspires us to know her Son. Doubt and despair can prevent this knowing, as they lead to mistrust. Jesus needs us to trust him and welcome him into our darkest hour. Struggling through a hardship alone is like being in hell. I cannot imagine surviving a tragedy without God and the prayers of family and friends. There are people trapped in despair and negativity, a hell-like state. Hell is the absence of God: the absence of love, beauty, truth and goodness. It is the opposite of hope. When Adam and Eve sinned and disobeyed God, they lost the comfort of God's home. Outside of God's love and God's will there is struggle and turmoil; this is why Adam and Eve were told that they would labour and sweat for the rest of their lives.

Knowing Christ relieves the burden: "Come to me, all you that are weary and are carrying heavy burdens, and I will give you rest. Take my yoke upon you, and learn from me; for I am gentle and humble in heart, and you will find rest for your souls. For my yoke is easy, and my burden light" (Matthew 11:28-30). This is why we must evangelize – too many people choose the hard way, the way that leads to struggle and turmoil. We cannot control all crosses that come our way, but following Jesus can eliminate the ones we can control. Knowing Jesus helps us to discern between those crosses that require stamina and endurance, and those we were not meant to carry.

Conclusion

The New Evangelization comes up quite a bit in Catholic circles: in homilies, conferences, parishes, classrooms and lectures. At one forum I attended, a priest shared his experience at a conference on media and the New Evangelization. He mentioned that the presenter at that conference said that the First Evangelization and the New Evangelization can be summarized in two scripture passages:

1. First Evangelization: "Go therefore and make disciples of all nations, baptizing them in the name of the Father and of the Son and of the Holy Spirit." (Matthew 28:19)

2. New Evangelization: "I ask not only on behalf of these, but also on behalf of those who will believe in me through their word, that they may all be one. As you, Father, are in me and I am in you, may they also be in us, so that the world may believe that you have sent me. The glory that you have given me I have given them, so that they may be one, I in them and you in me, that they may become completely one, so that the world may know that you have sent me and have loved them even as you have loved me." (John 17:20-23)

In this prayer from John's Gospel, Jesus expresses his desire that we experience the same intimacy he shares with the Father. He came to show us the love of the Father and wants us to know God the same way he does. He wants us to know we are known and that we are loved. We are invited to share in the love he and the Father share. Participating in this divine love unites us and makes us one. For some, this may be a new revelation.

I would argue, however, that the New Evangelization requires the approach affirmed by both scriptural passages. We go out as disciples to bring Christ and this offer of divine love. We invite all people through witness and proclamation, but we need to experience the intimacy of this divine communion before we can propose it to others. We need to be made new. This is part of the newness of the New Evangelization. The New You will inspire the quest for newness in others. The New You is really Christ who is always present. In other words, the New You is Jesus Christ who is the same throughout eternity. You will retain your individuality and unique personality, but will be restored and become the best version of yourself. You will make Christ visible to others.

We need the sacraments to nourish and strengthen us. We need the fellowship that comes with initiation into a community of faith. We need the love of Christ. Have you experienced this great love? Have you asked to feel the love Jesus shares with the Father? It is this divine love that makes us one with the Trinity and with one another. This is the message Jesus affirmed in the two commandments we find in Hebrew Scriptures:

> You shall love the Lord your God with all your heart, and with all your soul, and with all your mind. This is the greatest and first commandment. And the second is like it: You shall love your neighbor as yourself. On these two commandments hang all the law and the prophets. (Matthew 26:36-40)

If we follow these two commandments, we will not break the other commandments. This is tough, but our happiness depends on it. Loving God with all of our hearts spills over into love of self and love of neighbour. We cannot love our neighbours if we do not love ourselves. If we focus on our limitations, vulnerabilities, inadequacies and past mistakes, we are not open to healing. Our pride will keep us focused on our gifts or weaknesses, leading to comparison, judgment and jealousy. A humble self-awareness opens us up to God's healing grace and seeing our neighbour as our brother.

Spiritual growth leads to intimacy with God and acceptance of God's will. Living outside of God's will leads to struggle and burden. This is made clear in the Book of Genesis, in the account of creation and the fall. Accepting God's will with peace and joy eases the burden and unites humanity. But we all need to be on the same page. As long as some people do not know the love of God and the need to love themselves and their neighbour, there will be struggle and conflict. We need to evangelize because our fulfillment and salvation depend on it. God loves us too much to leave us in an incomplete state. Jesus completes and perfects us.

REPROPOSING CHRIST AND OTHER GREAT MYSTERIES

On Pentecost Sunday, we not only celebrate the beginning of our Church, we celebrate the conquering of fear and being strengthened with gifts of the Holy Spirit. We celebrate the possibility of becoming the best version of ourselves. The Holy Spirit is the power of God's love and the power to heal, transform and restore. The New Evangelization is all about *re-proposing Christ* – not imposing Christ – to those who do not know him or who have drifted away from him. It is also about *re-proposing the best version of you through the re-proposing of salvation*. It is not until we know Christ through an intimate encounter that we can come to know what it means to be restored or divinized. Even those who know him may not know that the Holy Spirit can make them a sneak preview of Christ, the best version of themselves. While this may involve an intense process, it leads to freedom and liberation.

In his inaugural mass as pope on October 22, 1978, Saint John Paul II said in his homily, "Do not be afraid! Open wide the doors to Christ … Do not be afraid. Christ knows what is in man."

Jesus knows who we are and how we feel, what troubles us and what enslaves us. He reveals freedom and our final destiny. In the homily he gave at his inaugural mass on April 24, 2005, Pope Benedict XVI built on the encouraging and fearless words of his predecessor:

If we let Christ into our lives, we lose nothing, nothing, absolutely nothing of what makes life free, beautiful and great! ...No! Only in this friendship are the doors of life opened wide. Only in this friendship is the great potential of human existence truly revealed. Only in this friendship do we experience beauty and liberation ... Do not be afraid of Christ! He takes nothing away, and gives you everything.

This is why we continue to evangelize: in re-proposing Christ, we re-propose the possibility of becoming a new creation. To know the intimacy that Jesus experiences with the Father and the Holy Spirit is the desire God has for us. God's love is not a distant love, but an intimate love that heals and transforms. When we evangelize, we help people to know God, to know they are loved and they can be transformed. We are fighting against a culture that is tempting people to believe that they do not need God (LG, n. 16). St. Augustine, in his *Confessions,* lamented coming to know God later in life: "Late have I loved thee." Some of us may be late in loving God and late in listening to his will: "Late have I listened to thee." Have the courage to say yes to an encounter with Christ. Have the courage to say yes to be the best version of you, the new you, a new creation.

This newness brings authentic freedom. This whole process demands that we take the time to explore our roots, those influences that may work against our freedom, our strengths and weaknesses, our upbringing, genetic history and more. Jesus mirrors back to us wholeness and "divine health." He is not limited by the factors that shaped us. Surrender all to Christ and invest in your spiritual future. Conquer your fear and embrace hope. Just as Jesus revealed the Father, have the courage to reveal Jesus to the world!

"Do not let that hope die! Stake your lives on it! We are not the sum of our weaknesses and failures; we are the sum of the Father's love for us and our real capacity to become the image of his Son."
 BLESSED JOHN PAUL II, WORLD YOUTH DAY, SOLEMN MASS, JULY 28, 2002, DOWNSVIEW PARK, ONTARIO, CANADA

For Further Reading

United States Conference of Catholic Bishops, "New Evangelization" at http://www.usccb.org/beliefs-and-teachings/how-we-teach/new-evangelization/index.cfm

Cardinal Donald Wuerl, *New Evangelization: Passing on the Catholic Faith Today* (HUNTINGTON, IN: OUR SUNDAY VISITOR PUBLISHING, 2013)

Robert Barron, *Catholicism: The New Evangelization*, information at http://catholicismnewevangelization.com/

Joseph Stoutzenberger, *An Invitation to Catholic Faith: Exploring the Basics* (NEW LONDON, CT: TWENTY-THIRD PUBLICATIONS, 2013)

Josephine Lombardi, *Living with the Holy Spirit* (TORONTO: NOVALIS, 2011)

David Knight, *The Nuts and Bolts of Daily Spirituality* (NEW LONDON, CT: TWENTY-THIRD PUBLICATIONS, 2013)

Endnotes

1   Thomas à Kempis, *The Imitation of Christ* (New York: Doubleday, 1955).

2   Cardinal Donald Wuerl, *New Evangelization: Passing on the Catholic Faith Today* (Huntington, IN: Our Sunday Visitor), 90.

3   http://www.assistnews.net/Stories/2010/s10070019.htm.

4   Joseph Cardinal Ratzinger, "The New Evangelization. Building the Civilization of Love."

5   Wuerl, 89.

6   For a detailed study of the Church's understanding of salvation outside the Church, see Josephine Lombardi, *What Are They Saying About the Universal Salvific Will of God?* (Mahwah, NJ: Paulist Press, 2007).

7   See also the Declaration on Religious Liberty from the Second Vatican Council.

8   See Lombardi, *What Are They Saying About the Universal Salvific Will of God?*

9   See the *General Directory for Catechesis*, nn. 47–48.

10   Canadian Conference of Catholic Bishops, *On Good Soil: Pastoral Planning for Evangelization and Catechesis with Adults* (Ottawa: CCCB, 2009), 47. This book contains many practical suggestions for catechesis and evangelization at the parish and diocesan level.

11   See CCCB, *On Good Soil*, 48.

12   Wuerl, *New Evangelization*, 39.

13   Novalis Publishing has a *Living with…* series that is very affordable and accessible.

14   This will be explored in Chapter 6.

15   See Joseph Cardinal Ratzinger, Address to Catechists and Religion Teachers, December 12, 2000.

16   CCCB, *On Good Soil*, 76.

17   Ibid.

18   The Puebla Conference Document (1979). The Third Meeting of the Latin American Episcopal Conference.

19   See Statistics Canada: http://statcan.gc.ca.

20   See www.pewforum.org.

21   See Rick Hiemstra, "Leaving, Staying and Returning: An Executive Summary of Hemorrhaging Faith." www. hemorrhagingfaith.com.

22   John Allen Jr., "All Things Catholic," *National Catholic Reporter*, August 18, 2006 (ncrconline.org).

23   *Ad Limina* visit, June 22, 2012 (Address to Colombian Bishops).

24   Wuerl, *New Evangelization*, 17.

25   See *Ubicumque et Semper*, apostolic letter of Pope Benedict XVI, where he notes that in some traditionally Christian countries, some areas have become "almost completely de-Christianized" (2010).

26   See Pope Benedict XVI, *Ubicumque et Semper*, 2010.

27 The first two working documents can be found on the official Vatican website: www.vatican.va. They contain an outline of topics and tasks to be addressed by the synod.

28 These can be found on the official Vatican website: www.vatican.va.

29 From the unofficial English translation of the propositions.

30 Pope Benedict's video message for the launch of the initiative.

31 See the unofficial English translation of the propositions: www.vatican.va.

32 Ibid.

33 See Congregation for the Doctrine of the Faith, *Pastoral Recommendations for the Year of Faith*, 2012.

34 Pope Francis, "Swim Against the Tide," *Origins*, May 9, 2013, Vol. 43, No. 1, 1.

35 Pope Francis, "Apart from the Church, It is Not Possible to Find Jesus," *Origins*, May 9, 2013, Vol. 43, No. 1, 2.

36 John Allen Jr., "Pope Francis and the New Evangelization" (Address given to the Diocese of Hamilton), Monday, October 21, 2013.

37 Humility in leadership, Catholic Social Teaching, and mercy have been taught by many popes over the centuries. These are rooted in biblical truths.

38 See especially *Redemptoris Missio*, n. 42.

39 Father Robert Barron is the Rector-President of Mundelein Seminary, University of St. Mary of the Lake. In a YouTube video based on this address, Father Barron lists seven qualities of a great evangelizer: 1. Be in love with Jesus Christ. 2. Be filled with ardor. 3. Know the story of Israel. 4. Know the culture. 5. Love the great tradition. 6. Have a missionary heart. 7. Know and love the new media.

40 Patricia Treece, *The Sanctified Body* (New York: Doubleday, 1987).

41 See Don Everts and Doug Schaupp, *I Once Was Lost: What Post Modern Skeptics Taught Us About Their Path to Jesus.* (Downer's Grove, IL: InterVarsity Press, 2008).

42 James Fowler, *Stages of Faith: The Psychology of Human Development and the Quest for Meaning* (HarperSanFrancisco, 1995).

43 Everts and Schaupp, *I Once Was Lost*, 31.

44 See also James Fowler, *Stages of Faith.*

45 See Wuerl, *New Evangelization*, 56.

46 See my book *On Earth as it is in Heaven* (Novalis, 2010) for a commentary on doing God's will.

47 The use of media and social communications will be addressed in Chapter 6.

48 See Peter John Cameron, *Why Preach: Encountering Christ in God's Word* (San Francisco: Ignatius Press, 2009).

49 See Elizabeth Somer, *Eat Your Way to Happiness* (Buffalo, NY: Harlequin, 2010).

50 See *An Unpublished Manuscript on Purgatory*, author unknown (Baltimore, MD: Fatima House Publications, 2002), 69.

51   See Patricia Hughes Baumer, "Lay Preaching and Canon Law," in *Empowering a New Voice: A Lay Preaching Training Formation Manual* (Eden Prairie, MN: Partners in Preaching, 2002). See also canons 759 and 767.

52   See Apostolicam Actuositatem, the Decree on the Apostolate of the Laity (1965); Pope John Paul II, *Christifidelis Laici* (1988); and other documents published by the Congregation for the Doctrine of the Faith and national conferences of bishops.

53   Similar to some examples given in Scott Peck's book.

54   See the research of Dr. Norman Doidge in *The Brain that Changes Itself* (New York: Penguin Books, 2007).

55   See the work of Dr. Gerald May in *Addiction and Grace: Love and Spirituality in the Healing of Addictions* (New York: HarperOne, 2007).

56   Mission of the Redeemer Ministries in Canada offers workshops on the New Evangelization that address the properties of God's being and dominant transcendental languages.

57   Magisterial teaching refers to the teaching of the Magisterium, the bishops of the Church. There are different levels of teaching with different levels of authority.

58   ST 1 Q. 84 a. 6.

59   See Tim Wilson, "À l'Écoute de l'univers: An interview with Dr. Alfred Tomatis," *MusicWorks* 35 (Toronto, 1986/87).

60   Dr. Andrew Newberg and other neuroscientists have looked into the effects of sound on brain wiring.

61   Hamilton Health Sciences, *Helping Your Child Recover from a Concussion,* 2011. See also "Stepwise Return to Play," guidelines based on the Zurich Consensus Statement on Concussion in Sport (2008) and the Canadian Pediatric Society (www.cps.ca) and Think First Canada (www.thinkfirst.ca).

62   Edited by Douglas A. Gentile. Available at www.drdoug.org.

63   Ibid., 159.

64   Ibid., 163.

65   Ibid., 162.

66   Ibid., 166.

67   See Archbishop Aquila, "Forty Years of the Culture of Death," *Origins*, January 31, 2013, Vol. 42, No. 34, 537–541.

68   See April 24, 2013, www.spiritdaily.com.

69   Teaching of the *Catechism of the Catholic Church* on why the Word was made flesh, nn. 458–461.

70   Dr. Daniel Amen and others tell us that the brain changes when one falls in love. Additionally, hormones are released by both men and women when they are sexually intimate, leading to a bond. Premarital sex can lead to two people who are not well matched being prematurely bonded for an indefinite period of time. John Paul II, in *Familiaris Consortio*, cautioned that a total gift of self can take place only in marriage.

71   Dr. Gary Chapman, *The Five Love Languages: The Secret to Love that Lasts* (Chicago: Northfield Publishing, 2010).

72   See Father Carroll, SJ, "Congressional Testimony on Effects on Families of Current Immigration Policies," *Origins*, April 25, 2013, Vol. 42, No. 46, 732.

73   See www.cccb.ca

74   See Pontifical Council for Justice and Peace, "Reforming the International Financial and Monetary Systems," *Origins*, November 3, 2011, Vol. 41, No. 22, 341–349.

75   http://blog.mlive.com/muskegon_chronicle_extra/2007/01/nestle_raises_stakes_in_bottle.html.

76   See Colin Todunter, "Genetically Engineered 'Terminator Seeds': Death and Destruction of Agriculture." January 21, 2013, www. globalresearch.com.

77   Ibid.

78   Ryan Sturgeon and Patrick J. Morrissette, "A Qualitative Analysis of Suicide Ideation among Manitoban Farmers," *Canadian Journal of Counseling*, Vol. 44. No. 2, 192.

79   See Todunter, , "Genetically Engineered 'Terminator Seeds.'"

80   See "The Galileo Affair," www.vaticanobservatory.org.

81   M. Beauregard and V. Paquette, "Neural Correlates of a Mystical Experience in Carmelite Nuns," *Neuroscience Letters* Vol. 405, No. 3, 186–190.

82   Andrew B. Newberg, *Principles of Neurotheology* (Burlington, VT: Ashgate, 2010), 145.

83   See John Paul II, *Crossing the Threshold of Hope* (New York: Random House, 1994), 67.

84   Pontifical Council for Justice and Peace, "Reforming the International Financial and Monetary Systems," *Origins*, November 3, 2011, Vol. 41, No. 22, 348.

85   Ibid., 349.

86   See article by Sandro Magister dated November 10, 2011, www.chiesa.espressonline.it.

87   Pope Benedict XVI, *Caritas in Veritate*, "On Integral Human Development in Charity and Truth," 2009, no. 67.

88   This document represents the views of over 100 scholars of Islam and other new signatories. Almost 10,000 people have endorsed it. The document makes connections between Christianity and Islam and endorses peace and dialogue.

89   See Secretariat for Non-Christians, *Dialogue and Mission* (1984).

90   See March 19, 2013, www.economist.com.

91   See www.cccb.ca for a PDF version of the document and a summary for church bulletins. The document can be ordered through the CCCB.

92   Reginald Bibby, *The Emerging Millennials: How Canada's Newest Generation Is Responding to Change and Choice* (Project Canada Books, 2009).

93   From a conversation with a seminarian on the need to use media in their ministry.

94   Allocution given on January 24, 1969, to the Officers of the Catholic Association of Italian Journalists (UCSI), *L'Osservatore Romano*, 24 January 1969.

Study Guide

This study guide is intended to help you read Dr. Josephine Lombardi's *Disciples of All Nations* through a more personal lens. The focus of *Disciples of All Nations* is the New Evangelization, which is about our encounter with Jesus Christ. The first step in this encounter, Dr. Lombardi tells us, involves self-knowledge. This study guide therefore serves as a "map" that will allow you to use the book to deepen your own self-knowledge – both as an individual (me) and collectively (me as a member of the Christian community, or Church) – in the light of the New Evangelization.

The Structure of Each Chapter

This study guide will follow the chapter outline of *Disciples of All Nations.* To explore each chapter, you will find three sections in the study guide.

- The first section, "Some Background Information Before You Begin," will explain a few technical terms, or the origin of certain quotes.

- The second section, "Major Ideas to Watch for and Questions to Consider," will tease out the central themes of each chapter and open up any questions that follow from them.

- The third section, "You May Ask Yourself," poses some questions for personal reflection following from the material in the chapter.

Let's use this three-part framework to delve more deeply into *Disciples of All Nations.*

INTRODUCTION

Some background information before you begin:

• *Evangelii Nuntiandi,* **14** (p. 13): Section 14 of "Evangelization in the Modern World," an apostolic exhortation, or letter, that encourages a community of people to undertake a particular activity, written by Pope Paul VI in 1975. See page 30.

• *Lumen Gentium,* **17** (p. 13): Section 17 of "Light to the Nations," the Dogmatic Constitution on the Church; this was one of the two foundational documents on the nature of the Church produced during the Second Vatican Council (Vatican II), a gathering of the world's bishops that took place from 1962 to 1965. The council was called by Pope John XXIII to "open the windows of the Church."

Major ideas to watch for and questions to consider:

Disciples of All Nations begins with the question "Who do you think you are?" It is a pivotal question that applies to everyone who is interested in searching for the meaning of life.

• Self-knowledge is not just self-centredness. What do the saints have to tell us, on page 10, about some of the benefits of self-knowledge?

• Self-knowledge leads us to an encounter with Christ. This is a deep, transformative, "life-changing" encounter.

• The New Evangelization reminds us that we are loved by a God who desires trust and intimacy.

You may ask yourself:

• Who do I think I am? (Give that question some serious consideration as you begin to reflect on this book.)

• Have I ever had a life-changing experience or encounter? What made it so transformative for me?

• Do I trust God? Do I know God? Do I trust that God loves me and knows me?

Chapter 1

Evangelization

Some background information before you begin:

• **Post-synodal apostolic exhortation** *Evangelii Nuntiandi* (p. 19): we saw the last four words in the section on the Introduction, above. "Post-synodal" tells us that the apostolic exhortation was written and sent out after (and probably, to some extent, as a result of) Pope Paul's synod, or consultative meeting, with the bishops.

• *Instrumentum Laboris*, **n. 11** (p. 21): Section 11 of the "working instrument," or working document, on the New Evangelization.

• **Ecclesiology** (p. 22): a theological understanding of the nature of the Church.

• **Theological anthropology** (p. 22): a theological understanding of the nature of the human person.

Major ideas to watch for and questions to consider:

The focus of this chapter is to look specifically at evangelization. What does the term "evangelization" mean?

• Jesus is the source of all evangelization. The woman of Samaria (John 4:1-42) had a life-changing encounter with Jesus. She responded by sharing this good news with the people of her town. Having been evangelized – having encountered Jesus – she evangelized her own community.

• There is an adage in Latin that means "You cannot give what you do not have." The Church begins the work of evangelizing by evangelizing itself. To paraphrase a well-known saying, evangelization starts at home.

• The fruit of evangelization is salvation. The woman of Samaria was saved by her encounter with Jesus. The notion of salvation is explored throughout this book. What is one way in which salvation can be understood? One of the intriguing images of salvation that Lombardi uses is the image of "the restored self." "Not only do we re-propose Christ and his Gospel," she says, "we re-propose the gift of salvation: divine health, or *salus*" If you skip ahead to page 89 for a minute, you can read an interesting account of a firefighter who had a vision of his restored self.

• To evangelize, then, is to communicate an encounter that will leave a person transformed. How did the Second Vatican Council articulate this conviction?

• What is the distinction between the First Evangelization (which took place in the first century in the Middle East, and in the fifteenth century in the Americas) and the New Evangelization?

• Why do you suppose that, near the end of the chapter, the author is at pains to point out that religious freedom is to be respected and honoured in all missionary activity?

• Obviously, the question of salvation outside the Church is one that needs to be explored a little more deeply. This will be done in the following chapter.

You may ask yourself:

• What is the "Good News" for us as Christians? What would be "Good News" for me?

• How does the Church need to be evangelized?

• What does it mean to be saved? What would it mean for me to be saved? Can I imagine what my restored self might look like or feel like?

Chapter 2

THE TEACHING OF VATICAN II AND WHAT HAPPENED AFTER THE COUNCIL

Some background information before you begin:

• *Ad Gentes*, n. 7 (p. 27): Section 7 of the Second Vatican Council's Decree on the Missionary Activity of the Church (see p. 28).

• **Catechetical activity** (p. 29): the deepening of the faith life (through teaching about the content of the Christian Tradition) of those who have accepted the Good News of Jesus Christ.

• **Magisterium** (p. 31): the teaching authority of the Church.

Major ideas to watch for and questions to consider:

From the terms outlined above, you can probably already see the focus of this chapter: looking outside the Church to other faith traditions, and the missionary activity associated with bringing the Good News to those who have not yet heard it.

• Is there salvation outside the Church? In other words, can people of other faiths be saved? For centuries, the saying "*extra Ecclesiam nulla salus*" was the basic ruling: "outside the Church there is no salvation." The passage from *Lumen Gentium* on pages 27–28 outlines how at Vatican II, the Church moved beyond that position to a broader understanding of the saving mission of Jesus.

• What three elements comprise the Church's evangelizing mission? There is always a need for ongoing missionary activity. Evangelization is a basic duty of the People of God.

• "Interior renewal" reveals an awareness of one's own responsibility for preaching and spreading the Gospel. What needs to happen before we can bring Christ to others?

• What are the three levels of evangelization outlined in *Evangelii Nuntiandi?*

• Missionary activity is most clearly associated with the first level.

The gospel is brought to non-Christians so that they may know Jesus Christ, the true face of God. This is the First Evangelization.

• Both missionary and catechetical activity are connected with the second level. This is where the New Evangelization is needed for those whose faith has become stale, lukewarm, without any life. The New Evangelization seeks to deepen their faith, but most importantly, it seeks to re-propose the gospel of Jesus so that people can rediscover the joy of his presence.

• Finally, the third level is characterized by ongoing catechetical and pastoral activity. The goal of catechetical activity is "to deepen the individual's relationship with Jesus Christ in and through the Church. This is best described as an apprenticeship in the Christian life."

• What are the four pillars of formation that should be included in any plan to catechize and minister to people who have accepted the faith?

• What does Pope Francis name in *Evangelii Gaudium* as three evils that lead to the decline of joy in our communities?

• What's new about the New Evangelization?

• What did Cardinal Ratzinger (who became Pope Benedict XVI) list as the four essentials of the right content of our faith?

• What else is "new" in the New Evangelization? And what is not new?

• The New Evangelization means an appropriate response to the signs of the times, to the needs of people living in today's social and cultural context. The next chapter will examine this context in greater detail.

You may ask yourself:

• What do I believe about the possibility of being saved for those outside the Church? Does a person need to have an explicit knowledge of God to go to heaven?

• How do I need to be evangelized, so that I might begin to bring Christ to others?

Chapter 3

DEMOGRAPHICS AND EVANGELIZATION

Some background information before you begin:

• **Demographics** (p. 41): the statistical data of a population, especially data showing average age, income, education, etc.

Major ideas to watch for and questions to consider:

This chapter is more about facts than Church teaching. In view of that, the following questions are posed to invite you to explore some of the key data that are being looked at:

• What are some of the indicators of the cultural and demographic shifts that have occurred in the Church over the past century?

• What's the difference between "affiliation" or "identification" vs. "practice" or "participation" with regard to religious observance?

• What percentage of the global population is Christian? What percentage is Catholic?

• What is happening in the Catholic Church in Latin America that makes it a particular focus for the New Evangelization?

• Why did Pope Benedict believe that Catholics were converting to other religious traditions?

• What did he suggest as a strategy to respond to this process?

You may ask yourself:

• How would I describe in my own words the changes taking place in the Church?

• What do these changes mean for the future of Christianity and for the Catholic Church?

Chapter 4

PAPAL TEACHING ON THE NEW EVANGELIZATION

Some background information before you begin:

• **Agnosticism** (p. 51): a belief that no one can know with certainty about the existence of God.

• **Ongoing catechesis** (p. 55): the process of deepening one's faith through learning; working towards "a clear understanding of the faith" (p. 55).

Major ideas to watch for and questions to consider:

The purpose of this chapter is to present a brief overview of how the New Evangelization has been addressed in papal teaching over the past half-century. This material is predominantly historical, so once again, looking for the answers to the questions below is one way to deepen your understanding of it:

• It is worth noting that Pope Paul's (by now familiar) apostolic exhortation *Evangelii Nuntiandi* underlines a theme that we are becoming used to hearing: Interior transformation is the aim of evangelization; the liberation from all that which enslaves us is part of what it means to be saved.

• Which pope laid the foundations for the New Evangelization?

• Which of the popes "can rightfully be considered the father of the New Evangelization"?

• When did he first use the term "the New Evangelization"?

• Which demographic data that we saw in the previous chapter might have prompted Pope John Paul II's statement that "The reality of a 'Christian society' which, amid all the frailties which have always marked human life is now gone"?

• Is the scope of evangelization limited purely to the Catholic Church?

• What is Pope Benedict's role in the New Evangelization?

• What is meant by the image of the "Courtyard of the Gentiles"? What does it mean in practical terms for the Church?

• What does Pope Benedict mean by "The Door of Faith"?

• How is Pope Francis' evangelization characterized?

You may ask yourself:

• What would I say to a non-believer who asks what the New Evangelization is all about?

• What technologies do I think Pope Benedict had in mind when he encouraged "the use of modern communications to promote the New Evangelization"?

Chapter 5

Witness and Proclamation: Seeing Salvation

Some background information before you begin:

• **Skeptics** (p. 63): people who doubt the truth of a religion, especially Christianity, or the truth of important elements of a religion.

Major ideas to watch for and questions to consider:

• The first form of evangelization is witness, which means having experienced an encounter with Christ and being transformed as a result. We saw the woman of Samaria as one example, and we could certainly point to St. Paul as a witness with whom we are all familiar.

• The words of Pope Paul VI in the text box on page 60 are familiar to anyone who is a teacher. As I read them, however, I am struck by how accurately they seem to describe the impact that Pope Francis had in his first year as pope. An example of the evangelizing power of witness ...

• This section on witnessing reminds us once again that the person who evangelizes must be himself or herself evangelized and converted. Our witness – the way we live as one who has been transformed by an encounter with Jesus – will speak to others of Christ. In other words, as Josephine Lombardi puts it, "You are the billboard for the message of the New Evangelization: salvation."

• The theme of holiness, or sanctity, is explored in a number of places in this book, and we will come back to it in later chapters. But some of the qualities that are characteristic of an authentic witness, from Patricia Treece's book on the "secret" of sanctity, are listed on pages 62 to 63. As part of our own deepening of self-knowledge, they bear looking at and reflecting on.

• One of the realizations you may come to is that people are not just born with these desirable qualities; they are the fruit of personal growth in faith. Lombardi taps into the research of Don Everts and Doug Schaupp, who studied the conversion from skepticism to faith. In their work, they outline five important shifts that a person experiences on the way towards conversion – or to put it another way, five stages from witness to proclamation. What are these five stages?

• There are some interesting reflections on the third stage that bear on our theme of self-knowledge. St. Teresa of Avila, who lived in the sixteenth century, reminds us of the basic importance of self-knowledge to our own development. The section on the "Dove Sketches" is particularly intriguing, because it gives us an inside look at how we see ourselves, in contrast to the more accurate vision that others have. And if we can be seen more truly by others, the children of God, how much more accurately – and compassionately – are we seen by God's very self?

• In light of this, which sacrament does it make perfect sense to look upon, as Cardinal Timothy Dolan proposed to the Synod on the New Evangelization, as the "sacrament of the New Evangelization"?

• The title of this chapter is "Witness and Proclamation." Thus far we have been looking at the first of those terms. It's time to move on to the second. What do we mean by "Proclamation"?

• Preaching is one form of proclamation. It can be experienced as an encounter that begins in human experience.

• For lay persons, the predominant experience of preaching is receiving the Word, as the disciples did on the road to Emmaus. But proclamation can be offered as well as received. The Church allows for lay preaching in certain contexts, and there are opportunities for qualified, faith-filled lay people to preach: "The Second Vatican Council not only affirmed the universal call to holiness regardless of state of life, it affirmed the gifts of the laity and encouraged lay people to contribute their gifts to the Church and to use their faith to evangelize in their homes and workplaces" (p. 77).

• One of the great gifts of the role of educator in a Catholic school or catechist in a parish is that the teacher or catechist evangelizes by using their gifts to show that they are people of faith.

You may ask yourself:

• How do I manifest, in my own life, the stages on the way to conversion?

• How well do I think I can see myself as "healed with the acceptance of God's love and self-knowledge"?

• Have I, as a lay person, ever had the opportunity to preach? What was my experience? If I haven't had this opportunity, how would I respond to it in future?

Chapter 6

AREAS OF OUR SOCIETY THAT NEED
AN ENCOUNTER WITH JESUS CHRIST

Some background information before you begin:

• **The Immaculate Conception of Mary** (p. 83): This is a very familiar term, and yet is often confused with the virginal conception of Jesus. The Immaculate Conception of Mary refers to the Church's understanding that as the mother of Jesus, and therefore the Mother of God, Mary was unique among human beings in being conceived without original sin.

• **The Assumption of Mary** (p. 83): This term means that God honoured the mother of his Son by sparing her the corruption of death and bringing her body and soul into heaven to be with her Son and Lord for all eternity.

• **Neuroscience** (p. 113): any of the sciences, such as neurochemistry and experimental psychology, that deal with the structure or function of the nervous system and brain.

• **Neurotheology** (p. 113): also known as spiritual neuroscience, neurotheology attempts to explain religious experience and behaviour in neuroscientific terms.

Major ideas to watch for and questions to consider:

The working document for the synod on the New Evangelization lists seven sectors in need of an encounter with Christ. This is the longest chapter in *Disciples of All Nations*, as it explores each of these sectors. Focus on the one or two sectors that most interest you, or to which you are most closely tied:

1. **CULTURE:** What are the idols in today's culture that keep us from knowing God? This is a key question in understanding the obstacles to evangelization. There are so many ways that we can be diverted

from spiritual growth, from the road to human wholeness. What are the three major ways in which we can encounter God? Each of these is looked at in turn. For each, in keeping with our focus on self-knowledge, I would like to pose a question:

• What kinds of people are most likely to encounter God as Truth?

• Through what kinds of people, or in what sorts of activities, do we encounter God as Beauty?

• Which qualities reflect Goodness? Which ones do not?

We began looking at personal sanctity in the previous chapter. There are some very rich sections in this chapter as well that can help us to understand what it means to be holy from a personal perspective. The examination of conscience on pages 93 to 96 is a good example.

2. SOCIAL SECTOR: What kinds of people are addressed in this sector? Lombardi comments on the marked difference in formation provided for those preparing for ordination to the diaconate and the priesthood, as opposed to the great majority of people preparing for marriage. It's a telling point. Families need support and need to feel part of a community. Communication in relationships is a key area, and is examined here in some detail. Immigration policies are another area that might be explored; these are the institutional expressions of what we practise about love of our neighbour. It is important to remember, as the author points out, that immigrants are family members as well; the family is the domestic church and is in need of healing and support.

3. THE ECONOMY: Through its social teaching, the Church has said and written a great deal about the increase in the gap between the rich and the poor, the inequality associated with the distribution of the world's resources, and the exploitation of God's creation. In a succinct but precise manner, Lombardi puts her finger on a few of the pressure points where economic justice is clearly wanting. The future in these areas does not seem to be hopeful.

4. TECHNOLOGY AND SCIENTIFIC RESEARCH: This sector examines the relationship between science and faith. What is the most visible sign of the Church's engagement in scientific research and advocacy? There was a time not so long ago when science and faith seemed to be at odds with one another, but as time goes on, and science finds out more about the intricate and wondrous workings of the universe, there seems to be a lot more room for fruitful discussion between science and theology. What two specific examples does Lombardi offer that are of particular interest to her? Science can give us the means to deepen our understanding of what we believe.

5. CIVIC LIFE: As can be seen from the list of areas included in this sector (see the text box on p. 114), it is very broad. The working document for the Synod of the New Evangelization emphasizes "a variety of urgent situations" that need to be addressed, including a commitment to peace; liberation of peoples; regulation and interaction of national governments; dialogue between different cultures and religions; defence of human rights and peoples, ethnic minorities and the most vulnerable; and integrity of creation and a commitment to the future of our planet. In this section of the chapter, each of these is touched on briefly. This is another sector where Catholic Social Teaching has a great deal of wisdom and insight to offer.

6. MEDIA AND SOCIAL COMMUNICATIONS: The working document for the synod on the New Evangelization insists on the need for devising "new tools and new expressions" to ensure that the gospel is better communicated. What two goals should guide our efforts in using the media and social communications to spread the gospel message?

7. RELIGION: It seems funny, in a way, to see Religion as a sector in need of an encounter with Christ. But this goes back to our principle that "in order to be an evangelizer, one must first be evangelized." We are called to an adult faith. It is up to the baptized to go out and evangelize. Pope Francis points out that the Church is not a babysitter. How can we encourage and inspire a "spiritual reawakening" and "reanimation" of baptized Catholics? We need to work towards giving individuals a sense of meaning in their lives. In terms of catechesis, the encounter with Jesus is central. Catechesis is a communal experience; not only does it require nurturing and time, it also requires trusting other Christians and fellowship. Mass attendance is another important matter. Without the Eucharist, we are spiritually malnourished. In the final section on "God's Curriculum," there is a wonderful series of questions on page 132 that offers a rich basis for reflection, and further material for our growing sense of self-knowledge.

You may ask yourself:

• Am I a truth-seeker? What obstacles do I encounter on this path?

• Am I a lover of beauty? In what ways can I share my gifts?

• Am I a sign of goodness? Can I substitute my name into the text of 1 Corinthians 13? Does it describe me?

• How do I stack up against the recommendations of Jesus and Paul on pages 100 and 101?

• From the very brief presentation of Dr. Gary Chapman's work on "The Five Love Languages" (p. 101), can I pinpoint my primary love language? That of my partner, if I am in a permanent relationship?

• Am I hopeful that global economic systems can change for the better, or do I feel that power and wealth will continue to be concentrated in the hands of fewer and fewer people?

• What is my instinctive response to science and technology – curiosity or mistrust? Do I think it is possible for science and faith to work together to mutually inform each other?

• What do I think about neurotheology: the field of study cited on page 113 and following?

• Among the list of aspects included in "Civic Life," is there one or more for which I have a personal passion, or about which I feel somewhat knowledgeable?

• What do I think might be some of the "new tools and new expressions" that could be used in the New Evangelization?

• How do I feel I stack up against the checklist of virtues on page 131, and the questions on page 132?

Chapter 7

MARY, THE STAR OF THE NEW EVANGELIZATION

Major ideas to watch for and questions to consider:

• Pope John Paul II referred to Mary as the Star of the New Evangelization, and Pope Benedict entrusted the Synod's work to her. The same outpouring of the Holy Spirit that was given to Mary will guide us as well. What does it mean to say that there is a "Marian 'style'" to the Church's work of evangelization?

• The Holy Spirit makes us another Christ, but there is a process involved: we need to be open to the process of transformation and sanctification.

• We are reminded that hope is the remedy where there is fear and discouragement. "The next time you are tempted to despair or are agitated, know that this is not of God. Pray to be released from this falsehood and to feel truth, the language of the Holy Spirit" (p. 135). Mary is the model of hope and resilience.

• On pages 136 to 140, we find more rich resources for personal reflection in the sections entitled "Obstacles to Hope" and "Helps to Hope."

• To be without hope, Lombardi tells us, is to be in a "hell-like state." Hell is the absence of God: the absence of love, beauty, truth and goodness. It is the opposite of hope.

• I love the closing words of this chapter: "Knowing Jesus helps us to discern between those crosses that require stamina and endurance, and those we were not meant to carry."

You may ask yourself:

• When am I tempted to doubt God's plan for me? How can spending time with the reflection on hope (pp. 136 to 140) help me overcome doubt?

• Am I aware of the crosses in my life that I am called to endure, and those that I am not meant to carry?

CONCLUSION

Major ideas to watch for and questions to consider:

• In the New Evangelization, Lombardi contends, as in the First Evangelization, we go out as disciples to bring Christ and the offer of divine love to people. We invite all people through witness and proclamation; however, we need to experience the intimacy of this divine communion before we can propose it to others.

• Loving God with all our hearts spills over into love of neighbour, and also love of self. A humble self-awareness opens us up to God's healing grace and to seeing our neighbour as our brother and sister.

• We need to evangelize because our fulfillment and salvation depend on it.

• The New Evangelization is all about re-proposing Christ – to those who do not know him or to those who should know him. It is also about re-proposing the best version of you through the re-proposing of salvation.

• This is why we continue to evangelize: in re-proposing Christ, we re-propose the possibility of becoming a new creation.

You may ask yourself:

• Have I experienced the love of Christ? How?

• Have I asked to share the love that Jesus shares with the Father?

I hope this Study Guide has been a help to you in deepening not only your understanding of the material found in *Disciples of All Nations*, but also your understanding of yourself, both as a believer and as a member of the Church, the Christian community, from which the New Evangelization extends.

May you come to know your "restored self" in the ongoing process of encountering Jesus and sharing that transformative encounter with others in a way that is meaningfully life-giving for them.

PAUL BEAUDETTE

Program Leader, Religion and Family Life
Hamilton-Wentworth Catholic District
School Board, Ontario